SEO

FOR BUSINESS

THE ULTIMATE BUSINESS-OWNER'S GUIDE TO SEARCH ENGINE OPTIMIZATION

R.L. Adams

Copyright © 2011 R.L. Adams

All rights reserved.

ISBN-10: 1502901099
ISBN-13: 978-1502901095

All Rights Reserved

Copyright © 2014 R.L. Adams. All rights are reserved, including the right to reproduce this book or portions thereof, in any form. You may not distribute this book in any way. No part of this text may be reproduced, transmitted, downloaded, decompiled, reverse engineered, or stored in or introduced into any information storage retrieval system, in any form or by any means, whether electronic or mechanical without the express written permission of the author. The scanning, uploading and distribution of this book via the Internet or via any other means without the permission of the publisher is illegal and punishable by law. Please purchase only authorized electronic editions, and do not participate in or encourage electronic piracy of copyrighted materials.

FTC & Legal Notices

The Author was complete as possible in the creation of this book. The contents within are accurate and up to date at the time of writing however the Author accepts that due to the rapidly changing nature of the Internet some information may not be fully up to the date at the time of reading. Whilst all attempts have been made to verify information provided in this publication, the Author assumes no responsibility for errors, omissions, or contrary interpretation of the subject matter herein. Any perceived slights of specific people or organizations are unintentional. There are affiliate links to products and services in this guide. The author will get paid if you purchase some of the products or services recommended as links within the content of this book. The author was not prepaid to recommend any of the products or services listed in this book but will generate an income, whether fixed, or recurring, on some of the links listed in this book.

TABLE OF CONTENTS

SEO University?...7
Introduction..12

1..15
   Getting Started...15
   Localized SEO Approach 18
   Content Marketing..20
   Understanding the Sales Funnel..22
   What is a Prospect?..26
   Finding Prospects..31
   Converting Prospects into Leads...37
   Converting Leads into Sales..42

2..45
   Marketing Fundamentals..45
   Website Optimized for SEO..50
   Content Optimized for SEO 62
   Sales Funnel with Opt-In Incentive 67
   Email-Based Campaigns..71
   Purchase, Review, Refer..77

3..80
   Local SEO 80
   Business Listings...83
   Online Reviews..89

4..92
   Content Marketing..92
   Step 1: Research Long-Tail Keywords 95
   Step 2: Create a Content-Marketing Strategy.......................99
   Step 3: How to Build Excellent Content to Market.......... 103
   Building Authority in Content Marketing......................... 111

5... 115

Building a Sales Funnel 115
Step #1 – Setup Email System 120
Step #2 – Build your Free Offer 122
Step #3 – Building Content 124
Step #4 – Building your Autoresponders 126

6 129
SEO for Business 129
5 Principles to Selling Anything 132

7 137
Social Media Marketing 137
Building a Social Media Strategy 139

8 145
Video Marketing 145
Video Marketing Strategy 148

9 151
Succeeding with SEO 151

Other Courses 154

SEO UNIVERSITY?

Welcome back to the SEO University. This is the third installment of courses available in the field of search engine optimization. In this course, we'll address some important strategies and techniques specifically designed for marketing businesses on the Web. Whether you're a sole proprietor, a partnership, a corporation, a non-profit organization, or any other kind of business offering any type of goods, products, services, or information, anywhere in the world, this course has been specifically designed to help you navigate the stormy online waters of Business SEO on the Web. Whatever you market or sell, this course will help you to laser-target your SEO approach to concentrate your efforts in the areas that will be the most beneficial for you.

This course builds upon prior courses and the knowledge presented therein. The fundamentals that were presented in the *SEO Fundamentals* course, and the strategies and tactics that were illuminated in the *SEO*

Strategies & Tactics course are both vital prerequisites for the knowledge contained in this course. If you haven't yet absorbed the material in those courses, then go back and do so now. SEO requires a highly diverse skillset in order to make significant improvements in ranking. And, without understanding the fundamental principles involved with SEO along with their application in real-world strategies and tactics, you won't have the foundational knowledge required to market and promote your business through SEO like a seasoned professional.

However, *SEO for Business* doesn't just solely focus on search engine optimization. This course has been particularly designed to help you in multiple areas of marketing your business on the Internet. In fact, this course has been designed specifically to assist you in multiple areas of Internet Marketing when it comes to any type of business. No matter what you're peddling, big or small, local or global, cheap or expensive, this course will help guide you in developing a marketing strategy that works. Upon completion of this course, you'll have a complete scope of understanding for just how to drive traffic organically using localized SEO, building content marketing that works, building sales funnels with landing pages, conducting email-marketing campaigns, and converting browsers into buyers. You won't find any other comprehensive course that packs the same kind of value-punch for this type of content, as *SEO for* Business does, anywhere on the Web.

The information contained herein is going to be central in your efforts to driving traffic and converting leads to sales, so be sure to pay careful attention. Furthermore, I'll say it again, if you haven't yet gone through the prior two courses, now is the time to do so. Be sure that you have the foundational knowledge that's delivered in those courses so that you can best take advantage of the information contained in this particular course. Otherwise, you might feel a little bit lost at times.

So, here's an overview of just what we'll be covering in the pages of this course.

- Local SEO – This course builds on the prior knowledge presented in the past two courses by offering a localized SEO approach. We'll look at the specific techniques involved for building a local brand profile for your business, along with the steps required to help give your business an immediate presence in your area. This information is terrific if your products, services, or information are focused around a city, state, or even locale. For example, if you provide real estate services in a certain county or region, sell insurance in specific states, and so on, then this information is going to be vital to you.

- Content Marketing – When it comes to SEO for business, the name of the game is content marketing. We briefly covered some of this ground in past courses, but here, we'll discuss specifically how to use content marketing to generate traffic, buzz, leads, and sales for your business. We'll cover things like, just what to market, where to market it, and the best practices in doing so. We'll cover strategies that work and just how to institute them to best increase your presence on the Web.

- Email Marketing – Although SEO is paramount to running any business on the Web, email marketing is what's going to drive your message home and convert those browsers into buyers. In this section, we'll cover just what it takes to setup an email marketing campaign that will automatically communicate with your visitors and just how to entice them into providing you with their email address.

- Sales Funnels – We'll look at what a sales funnel is and just how to build one to help drive your business from organic search through lead and into a sale. Sales funnels, when configured properly, can help fuel your business no matter what it is you're selling on the Web. And, by properly configuring the right funnel, you'll enjoy a steady stream of sales on autopilot.

- SEO for Business – We'll look at just how to configure your business with SEO and what steps are vital in helping to catapult you in front of the eyes of searchers looking for your goods, services, or information. Whether you have a brand new domain or not, we'll discuss strategies that will help to drive traffic to your business now while building up your domain's authority over time.

- Social Media Marketing – This is a vital component to any marketing campaign on the Web. Understanding social media and its integration with SEO for your business is going to be paramount to your success. We'll cover the major components involved in weaving together a successful social media marketing campaign and just how to effectively market to your friends, fans, or followers on the Web.

- <u>Video Marketing</u> – Video is one of the most effective tools in SEO and overall marketing for businesses on the Web, and we'll look at how to effectively leverage video platforms like YouTube to propel your business forward. The video platform is one that can help catapult any business, new or old, into the forefront of the mainstream. And, properly leveraging this platform is going to be one of the critical steps in marketing and promoting your business on the Web. We'll address what works and how to deploy strategies and tactics that will be an effective usage of your time.

R.L. ADAMS

INTRODUCTION

SEO for Business is a course designed to help you take your business marketing to the next level. From the ground up, this course provides you with the information and the tools necessary to market any business on the Web like a seasoned professional. Built upon the foundation of knowledge presented in the prior two courses of the SEO University, *SEO for Business* will help to propel your sales into the stratosphere by understanding localized SEO and content marketing, driving targeted traffic to your offers, generating leads, and converting leads to sales. Look, we all know how difficult marketing in the real world can be. We can read all the theory that we want but when it comes down to it, we want actual methods and techniques that are going to get us sales. And that's what this course is specifically designed to do.

Of course, there are no guarantees of anything here. Although I've designed this course with the most up-to-date information available in industry, times do quickly change. What's most important is that you consistently do the work to promote and increase your PageRank over time while also improving your sales funnel along the way. Sales funnel? Well, I know that term might sound confusing to you right now, but it's just a fancy word for a system that will help filter (or funnel) leads into your database that you can eventually convert to paying customers. Sales funnels are one of the most critical elements for businesses that must exist to properly capitalize on your traffic. Whether you're driving organic traffic or paid traffic, that traffic is going to be worthless if there's no system in place to turn that traffic into real actualized dollars, pounds, euros, or any other currency in the world.

No matter where you're reading or listening to these words from around the world, as long as you adhere to the principles discussed in this course and the prior courses, then no matter what you're selling, you'll be able to increase your exposure and your bottom line. Marketing on the Internet is hard because driving organic search traffic to your offers is hard. Unless you know what you're doing and you specifically incline your offers and your funnel to capitalize on the traffic you do receive, you'll be wasting your time and spinning your wheels. Don't allow that to happen. Take the time to set things up properly from the outset and don't be afraid to buckle down and do the work. And, if you're afraid of doing the work, then you might as well kiss those sales goodbye, because this is going to take some nose-to-the-grindstone effort. But, nothing in life that's worthwhile will come easy, right? If it was easy, don't you think everyone would be doing it? Of course they would be.

So, get organized and be detail-oriented in your approach. The more you can do these two things, the better your chances are going to be for success in the long haul. Also, it's important to not get discouraged when it comes to SEO. There's a lot of knowledge to absorb and grasp and if you've already been through the prior two courses, then you've come a long way. But, there's so much more to learn when it comes to marketing. The full picture for organically marketing any business on the Web goes beyond just SEO. Successfully marketing a business on the Web stems into the Internet Marketing sphere where leads are converted to sales through specific tactics. But, you must first be able to drive the traffic to your site, capture the lead, and then make the sale. This isn't going to happen overnight. In fact, your initial setup will probably cause you some grief and frustration, so expect that. However, with a little bit of blood, sweat, and tears, you can build a business that will automatically drive traffic, capture leads, and convert sales without having to do much additional work.

The bulk of what you'll have to do lies in the initial setup. In this course, we'll be covering all of those initial steps to setting up your business from a marketing standpoint. There are so many elements to address at the outset that it's important to get things just right. It's not just about the organic search engine traffic; it's about what you do to capitalize on that search traffic. So, if you're ready to get started, then buckle in and let's get to it. There's a lot to cover in a short period and it's important that you do the work to absorb the information. If you don't understand something, take the time to go back and read or listen through it again. Once you do have a solid grasp on the information, then it's time to put that information into action. Be sure to go through the steps and configure things the right way the first time around. And most importantly: don't give up. The road to SEO dominance in business is a long one, but if you ensure that you make just a little bit of progress each and every day, you'll eventually reach all of your goals.

1
GETTING STARTED

So, where do we get started? If you've reached this course, then you have some SEO knowledge behind your belt. If you've gone through the prior two courses, which are prerequisites to this course, then you'll have the foundational knowledge to understand and implement certain strategies when it comes to marketing any business on the Web. If you didn't do those courses, then it's important to go back and do them now. Otherwise, you'll be entirely lost when it comes to multiple sections of this book. However, I'll assume that you did do the work presented in those courses and you have a solid grasp of the knowledge conveyed therein. So, where do we go from here then? Now that we understand the fundamentals and some of the strategies involved with SEO, why do we need *SEO for Business?* What's the difference between the knowledge presented in those courses, and what's available here?

Well, SEO in theory and in practice is one thing.

However, *SEO for Business* goes much further beyond that and into a marketing strategy that has SEO as merely one of its cornerstones. In this course, you're not only going to learn just how to implement SEO from a business standpoint, but you're also going to be exposed to the tools and techniques required to turn that traffic into real and actualized dollars. And, as you'll come to find within the sections of this course, this information is going to be vital to taking any business from concept to fruition on the Web. That's because we all need not only a good game plan when it comes to marketing on the Web, but we actually also need a roadmap too. Well, this is that roadmap. The information in this course will help you not only market your own business, but also learn the basic building blocks to successfully launching and promoting anyone's business on the Web. With this knowledge, you could sell your services and expertise to others for top dollar, or work on building your own businesses and streams of income.

Please also bear in mind that this course isn't about hype. There are no guarantees here that you're going to get rich by implementing the knowledge and information presented herein. If you've followed along with the SEO University up until this point, then you know this information is all about building a solid foundation for the future. Sure, there are ways to quicken the pace to profits, but oftentimes it's simply not worth the potential for risk and expenses that may be associated with it. So, be sure that you follow along and stick to a game plan. Consistently apply the knowledge that you learn, and never give up. Remember the cliché that Rome wasn't built in a day? Well, it wasn't, and your path to SEO prowess in the business world also won't come overnight. It's going to take endless hours of toil and struggle. But, once you do reach that pinnacle, then you'll most certainly reap the endless benefits of it.

So, considering that you have two courses under your belt at this point, then you should be well versed in the field of SEO. You should understand the fundamentals, basic principles, building-blocks of trust, advanced strategies, and just how to connect the dots when it comes to organically marketing any site on the Web through SEO. However, there's so much more to marketing a business on the Web than that. Sure, those are some of the precursors involved, which at times might seem a bit overwhelming, and it is. But, keep in mind, that there's much more involved. When we market from a business perspective, we're capitalizing on the traffic and capturing those leads to be able to eventually convert them to sales. So, *SEO for Business* goes beyond just mere optimization of your site for organic search rankings; *SEO for Business* is about optimizing your business for profits.

LOCALIZED SEO APPROACH

Although we've covered some significant ground in the past two courses on the fundamentals of SEO and the strategies involved, we didn't get into the specific aspects of marketing a real business on the Web. The need for real-world profits, and the slowness of real-world SEO advancement, go together like salt on a wound. When you start a new business, you need sales and profits. Yet, when you start a new business, and attempt to market it on the Web, you're likened to a man stranded in the middle of a vast sea trying to call out for help without a bullhorn. Unless you understand a quickened approach for getting the word out, you either have to have an enormous marketing budget, or an enormous amount of time to dig in your heels and grind.

Now, if we all had both time and money, we know that we wouldn't be approaching marketing primarily through SEO. We would be approaching marketing through paid advertising mediums such as through cost-per-click (CPC) or cost-per mile (CPM) advertising. Those types of advertising can be gauged based on their effectiveness through various means that include conversion tracking and sales. Instead, what we're attempting here is to organically saturate the market with our offer to the best of our ability without betting the farm. We all know that it's costly to market a business in the beginning, and with so many other seemingly-unrelated issues that call our attention in the business world, this can get frustrating very quickly, especially when sales are at a standstill.

This is why localized SEO is an important approach in the beginning. So, why localized SEO? And, what's the difference between general SEO and local SEO? Well, localized SEO is important for a number of reasons. The main reason being that, when conducting local SEO, your targeting naturally becomes more specific. From a term like "Web Design Services," for generalized SEO, to "Manhattan Beach Web Design Services," breeds that long-tail keyword that we've come to know in past courses of the *SEO University*.

So, local SEO is important because it works on building rank for organic search terms in a local area, which is far easier to do than building global rank for much harder keywords. So, the more specific you can get, the easier it will be for you to appear more relevant. And we all know that relevancy is the name of the game. So, instead of a broad approach, we're going to focus on a local approach here that will also leverage some of the popular services that exist on the Web. Examples would be Yelp, Google Local business listings, Yahoo Local, Angie's List, and so on. We're going to develop a local SEO strategy in this section, and begin honing in on just how we're going to target that business to gain rank locally. You'll find this much more satisfying in the time spent versus benefits received relationship of productivity output.

CONTENT MARKETING

One thing that we touched upon in past courses was content marketing. We spoke about some of the benefits of marketing content on authority sites, and even looked at some strategies involving it. However, content marketing for business involves numerous other facets that must come together in a coherent overall strategy that aims at building a value-based platform for a particular business or niche. This is the kind of content marketing that we're going to cover herein, and dive deep into building a framework of trust that will help to provide optimal boost for organic search rankings.

Although we'll still be utilizing pre-existing authority sites to do this, we'll look at specific blueprints on how you can leverage your niche or industry to take content marketing to the next level. We'll get into the details about what types of content work and what types don't. We'll look at utilizing trending data that can be spun into either authority content, or even infographics. We'll also see how best to utilize a calendar to optimize the distribution of content that's intended to drive traffic, build links, create leads, and eventually, result in sales.

We'll also look at the best type of content to develop and just how to implement a strategy to get the best results for your time spent. Because, at the end of the day, it really does just boil down to obtaining the widest reach possible for your site. The more people that like and share your content, the higher your PageRank will go, and the more organic search traffic you'll eventually receive. But this doesn't happen overnight. It takes consistent and repeated effort in building and marketing content that provides value.

And, no content marketing strategy for business is complete without also brushing up on social media marketing. Now, if you've never leveraged social media to market, now is the time to do so. Even if you don't want to share your business pages with friends, marketing through mediums like Facebook, Twitter, and LinkedIn are crucial for market saturation. We'll focus on what works here from a business standpoint, and cover some major ground while doing so.

UNDERSTANDING THE SALES FUNNEL

One of the most important concepts to grasp when marketing any business on the Web is the sales funnel. Sound like a strange term to you? Well, before long, you'll be educating people close to you about all the ins-and-outs of marketing a business on the Web, and you'll be using terms like *Sales Funnel, Squeeze Page,* and *Email Drip Rate* before you know it. But, understanding the sales funnel is likened to understanding the entire process that goes on from the point of initial contact with a prospect through whatever means, to the final sale. Now, everything that goes on between the point of initial contact with a customer, and the final sale, all occur with a sales funnel. A properly configured sales funnel can lead to a tremendous amount of sales.

If you think about a regular funnel for a moment, you most likely know that the top is wider than the bottom. And, if you were to dissect that funnel so that you could see through it, you would then see the various stages of the sales funnel. The sales funnel starts with the prospects, which are at the very top at the widest point. You can literally have thousands upon thousands of prospects that arrive at your Website. Now, we'll certainly be reviewing some specific strategies for marketing a business organically through SEO, but more importantly, we'll be reviewing just how to get that search traffic and convert them into paying customers. This is where the heart of marketing lies, and it's through an effective sales funnel that you'll be able to capture those leads and convert them into real actualized dollars.

So, the sales funnel starts with the prospects at the top that filter into the funnel. There will be many prospects that will ultimately come through the funnel, but not all of those prospects will make it down through all the various stages of the funnel. But how do they get into the sales funnel in the first place? Well, organic SEO is one such method but there are others such as social media, video tutorials, free giveaways, and blog posts that create tremendous amounts of value. We'll be going into detail about some of these, but it's important here to merely get an overview of the sales funnel, as this process is going to be at the heart of your marketing work. So, let's take a look at the various stages of the sales funnel and just how the process works:

1. Prospect traffic arrives at your Website through:

    a. Organic search traffic

    b. Social media traffic

    c. Syndicated blog articles

    d. Video marketing traffic

     e. Content marketing traffic

     f. Paid advertising traffic

2. Prospect traffic is converted into leads through:

     a. Freebies and Giveaways

     b. Email newsletter content

     c. Webinars

     d. Other incentives

3. Leads are converted to sales through:

     a. Email drip-campaigns

     b. Email newsletter campaigns

     c. Product or service trials

So, why is it important to understand how this entire process works? Well, as you may already know, whether you're in business for yourself or not, marketing on the Web takes a significant amount of effort. It's not just about driving traffic or posting links on social media. Once you do get the traffic there, you have to be able to convert. If you don't have the technical knowledge, then you could be wasting precious resources and losing your prospects. So, we have to capitalize on the traffic that does reach your site and we have to do it in the proper way. This is what *SEO for Business* is going to be about. From prospect, to lead, to customer, we'll go through the entire lifecycle of the sales funnel and just how to move those individuals successfully through from start to finish.

WHAT IS A PROSPECT?

So, we have some knowledge behind our belt. We know just how to drive organic search traffic through SEO to our site. We've also learned some strategies as they were discussed in the second course of the SEO University. But, what we never talked about was just who or what that visitor is that lands on your site. A prospect is someone who's showed enough interest to your content that they've found you through some means of online search and clicked through to your site. Maybe they found you through a link that was shared on social media, or maybe they found you through an organic search on Google or another search engine. But, whatever way they found you, they've somehow ended up at your Website. This individual, or prospect, is now reading your content and eye-scanning your site from left to right, top to bottom. Why is all of this important? Well, just what catches this prospect's eye and what makes him go from a prospect to a lead is critical.

So, in our quest to understand and engineer the perfect sales funnel, we'll be paying close attention to the prospect and just what he or she is doing on your site. We'll discuss what works and what doesn't when attempting to take that prospect to a lead, and later on, of course, through a sale. But we have to start somewhere. The prospect is going to expect certain things, just as Google expects certain things in order to make your listings appear in its coveted search results. So, we have to ensure that we engineer things the right way from the ground up in order to capitalize on the traffic we do get. When your sales funnel isn't configured properly, and your content or offers don't meet the vigorous eye-scanning tests that the prospect will put your site through, then your time could be literally wasted. Sure, it's great to have traffic coming to the site through organic means, but without taking that traffic and converting it into real dollars, time can be wasted if you're in the business of making money. And, even if you're blogging as a hobby, understanding how to generate passive income from your blogging is important.

At this point, blogging should be taking center stage for you. If you've gone through the first two courses of the SEO University then you know just how important it is to put out fresh content that's well-written, engaging, and provides value. And, when it comes to blogging for your business, it's okay to give away the farm in your content. Prospects love to absorb well-written content that helps to fill some need or answer some question.

But, why give away so much great content in your blogging? Do prospects really expect to get all the answers that they're looking for through your blog posts? The short answer to that question is yes. Prospects do expect to get the answers to their questions in your blog posts. And, the better your content can deliver those answers, the more likely you're going to turn those prospects into leads. Why is that? Well, when you can consistently deliver relevant information in an industry that fills some need or void, and you can do it in a well-written and engaging manner that adds value to peoples' lives, then you set yourself up as an authority.

What's the importance of being an authority? Well, if you'll recall back to our discussions in the past couple of courses, authority sites are one's that are well-trusted on the Web by search engines like Google. Similar to an authority site, when you're viewed as an authority in an industry or a field, people being to spread your content around and help to build authority for you. This is critical in the eyes of Google. When great content is shared, liked, re-tweeted, and so on, Google begins to take notice. It knows that well-written content that's engaging and adds value is going to be shared. And, Google wants to move that content up in its search rankings. So, delivering excellent content, and doing that consistently over time, will set you up as an authority. Being an authority brings with it so many benefits that extend beyond just a high ranking on Google's SERPs.

So, giving away the farm is important, but there's more to it than that. You don't want to just give away the farm and not be able to capitalize on the traffic that's coming through and eye-scanning your site. You have to turn those prospects into leads by offering something of greater value. And, in turn, you'll want to reap some benefits by offering that greater "thing" of value. What could that "thing" of value be? Well, it can be anything from an ebook, which is one of the most common forms, to some report with important information about the industry, or even access to some set of training videos. You see, that "thing" of value can be literally just about anything. But it must provide an enormous amount of value and it must entice prospects enough to give up their email addresses. Why do you want their email addresses? Well, we'll be embarking upon the road of email marketing in this course, and you'll come to find just how valuable those email addresses are going to be in the future to you.

Now, whether you're in a brick-and-mortar style business or an online business, you can provide something of great value that will entice people to give up their email addresses. These leads are going to be at the very top of your funnel. They are going to be the ones that you'll be marketing to on a periodic basis. Sound like a lot of work? Well, to an extent, it will be in the beginning. However, we're going to automate much of this process. What does this mean? Well, we'll get into email-drip campaigns and just how they work later on in this course. For now, it's important to understand and develop a strategy for capturing those email addresses. That's because those email addresses are going to be at the very heart of your business. And it will be through the cultivation of your relationship with those leads that will lead to wild profits in any field. But in the very beginning, it will be a tremendous amount of work and effort to capture those leads.

It's important to keep in mind, at this very early stage in the game, that those leads will be like gold and they should be treated as such. Never spam or over-contact your leads for risk of losing them as subscribers. And, you'll have to ensure that when you do contact them, that you're providing value and not just trying to sell at every step of the game. Why is this important? Well, just imagine it yourself and think about how you would feel if you were constantly being marketed to from an email list that you joined? It wouldn't feel too good. So, we'll get into the specifics of just what it's going to take and how often you should contact your leads. For now, the principles and fundamentals that we discussed in prior courses are going to apply. Just like Google wants to see you providing value through content, leads are also going to want to see that as well. When your leads see you consistently providing value to them through content, they will not only stay loyal, but they will also tell friends about you as well. So, always keep those fundamental principles in the back of your mind as they are going to universally apply to all that you do.

FINDING PROSPECTS

All of the work we covered in the prior two courses offers the basic building blocks for finding prospects on the Web. We learned so much about what it takes to optimize your site for search engines like Google, but *SEO for Business* is more of a laser-targeted approach to building your business on the Web. So, how do we go about finding prospects? Where are they lurking? Well, depending on your niche or industry, you'll most likely go about finding your prospects in different ways. However, there are a few staple approaches to find them on the Web. Of course, we've covered organic SEO and optimizing your articles for Google traffic. Things like content marketing, video marketing, social media marketing, and blogging are going to play a major role here. These are going to be the core components of your work in the field. But, getting the traffic to the site is only half the battle. Of course, the more difficult task is going to be in converting that traffic to leads, and subsequently, to sales.

So, overall, here are the primary ways in which you can find your prospects on the Web. They don't just include work that involves SEO, as they extend beyond that. What we're looking to do is go to where your potential clients are gathering. And, it's not too difficult to do this. No matter what industry we're talking about, there exist forums and blogs that are authorities in their respective niches. These should be one primary target for you at the outset. But, here's an overview of all that we need to target:

1. Organic search traffic – The organic search traffic will be one of the best and most passive-traffic sources that you can invest your time into. However, building up this stream of traffic is difficult and takes an excruciatingly long time. But, when you leverage the power of authority sites to build content, you can quicken this pace. Yet, this won't happen overnight. This is one of the most frustrating parts for business owners that are new to marketing on the Web. Most people are expecting overnight results but it just won't happen. This is why diversification is important when it comes to *SEO for Business*. If we were to put all of our time and effort into optimizing articles on your own domain, it would be difficult to drive traffic without constantly applying that effort over a very long period.

2. Social media traffic – Of course, we all know about the social media traffic and the importance of it. However, there are ways to market through social media when it comes to businesses and ways not to market. However, the fundamentals

will still apply here. We have to ensure that we're adding value through content that's both well-written and engaging, but we also can't constantly be cheerleading our products and/or services all of the time. Similar to organic searches, social media relationships and presence must be cultivated over time. It will take time to build and foster those relationships before you have a solid platform or foundation for growth. But, we all have to start somewhere.

3. Forum interaction traffic – This is an excellent way to both build the authority rank of your site while also helping to drive traffic. But, just like everything else, forum interaction must be done with tact. You can't simply jump onto the forums and start promoting and cheerleading your offers, or else they will fail. However, your success in this area also boils down to finding the right forums in your niche or industry. When you can locate the right forums, and you can help to provide value to other forum members, you can then post your own links from time to time. But, it's easy to get carried away with self-promoting in forums, so you must tread with care. Focus on helping answer other forum members' questions by engaging and adding value to conversations. This is one of the quickest ways to speed things along when it comes to both search engine traffic and real human visitors that are taking interest in whatever it is that you're peddling.

4. <u>Blog commenting traffic</u> – Another source for driving traffic and finding those prospects is by commenting on blog posts that have some authority in your industry or niche. Search out and find blogs that are providing tremendous amounts of value and start reading through the comments on the various articles. And, see if you can provide some value by responding to comment threads that you might be able to add something of interest to. Again, it's important that you don't merely attempt to sell here. Cheerleading or blatantly spamming links is likely to get you banned from commenting on those blogs again. But, in the least, it's likely to have those comments removed and your well-spent time would go to waste. Again, you have to tread a fine line here and cultivate relationships. Don't just try to sell, sell, sell at every turn of the corner. You won't get anywhere by doing solely that.

5. <u>Syndicated blog articles</u> – By syndicating your own blog articles, you can work on driving prospect traffic to your site. There are multiple methods for doing this that would include syndication networks, social bookmarking sites, and so on. Popular resources are sites like Reddit.com, Digg.com, StumbleUpon.com, and others. These are great ways of getting your content in front of droves of people. But, keep in mind that your content has to be well-written and provide tremendous amounts of value in order to be shared enough times to make a significant impact. Still, by leveraging these important Websites, you can ensure that as many potential eyes see your content as possible. We'll discuss just how to craft content for your business and market it in this

manner in order to drive prospects to your site.

6. Video marketing traffic – This is one of the most important avenues for driving traffic to your business that's largely untapped by many. Why? Well, most people shy away from online videos and tutorials. Yet, so many people are looking for video content that will help them solve a problem or fill a need. And, sites like YouTube.com and Vimeo.com have very high PageRanks, which makes sharing any useful content very beneficial to the producer of that content. This will be one of the primary strategies for driving traffic to your business with SEO. We'll discuss just how to construct that video to fit your specific niche or industry. We'll look at just what it's going to take in order to help build online videos that will drive prospects to your site and potentially convert them into leads and eventually paying customers.

7. Content marketing traffic – This will be one of the most important methods for, not only building PageRank, but also for spreading your message quickly. If you'll recall from the past course, content marketing involves posting high-quality well-written content on authority sites in an effort to draw in visitors. Authority sites help to draw in droves of visitors because they are at the forefront of millions of peoples' eyes. They are the sites that so many of us have become so accustomed to surfing through. So, content marketing traffic will be integral in your quest for drawing in prospects. And, the quality of your content marketing will aid you in turning those prospects into leads when

they click through to your site from those all-important authority sites.

8. Paid advertising traffic – Of course, in business, there's always the paid route. In the past two courses, we didn't discuss the paid advertising method since those courses were primarily organic SEO courses. However, in *SEO for Business*, paid advertising is a method that can be used to draw in visitors in an effort to capture those leads. We'll get into things like squeeze pages, social media ads, and other paid traffic sources that will assist you in driving traffic to your site that you can then capitalize in. However, since most people won't have a large budget for this, we'll get into the setup and testing of small ads to find what does work. Once we have our sales funnel in place and some test data, the sky is the limit with how we can scale this out. But, the front-end work will be tremendous before you can reach that point.

CONVERTING PROSPECTS INTO LEADS

The second vital part of the sales funnel is to convert your prospects into leads. Once the prospects arrive at the site, the likelihood of their conversion into leads is based on just how convincing your offer is. If your offer is convincing, then it will compel that prospect to give up his vital information. If your offer falls short, that prospect-traffic could be gone forever. Remember, email addresses should be treated like gold, as they're the most valuable resource that you'll build up in your quest to build an online business. Prospects won't just give up their email addresses on a whim. They have to have a very good reason why they should relinquish their information to you. If you can convince them to do so, then you've completed one of the major hurdles involved with building a successful sales funnel.

But, the goal shouldn't just be email-extraction. You must base your business on the foundational principles of trust discussed in the first course. Primarily, what we're talking about here is trust in content. Content is king and information is power. So, if you have the right content and the right information, then you have the power. That information should provide tremendous amounts of value. Why else would people relinquish their contact details to you? Why else would someone give up their email address and risk receiving spam from one more sources on the Web? They shouldn't have to risk anything. Your job is going to be to ensure them that they have absolutely nothing to lose by providing their contact details, and absolutely everything to gain. This is where your offer comes into play and where you'll be converting your prospects into leads.

So, what are the ways in which we can make our sites and offers appealing enough to convert those prospects into leads? How are we to compel people to give up their vital details and to do it with confidence? Well, by establishing yourself as an authority in any niche or industry and providing information-rich content that you would then giveaway free would be one of the most expeditious routes. However, we can't all become authorities in our respective industries overnight. And, becoming an authority takes a significant amount of work. However, you can begin making strides towards that right now by building valuable content that you would then give away free in exchange for that all-important email address and contact information.

In short, these are all the methods that we'll be covering for converting prospects into leads:

1. <u>Freebies and Giveaways</u> – This is the most popular method for converting prospects into leads. You've most likely seen this on other blogs

that you've visited in your quest to find answers to your questions through online searches. These generally tend to come in the form of either a pop-up email-signup box when you land on the blog, or a form in the sidebar. The former method is a bit more invasive but some find it far more effective. Some people don't like to be hit with a popup email signup box when they land on a blog looking for some information they were searching for the answer for. I would most certainly recommend the latter method of having the signup form with freebie or giveaway in the sidebar. Now, you might be thinking, "What am I supposed to be giving away?" Well, this is where you have to get creative. We'll discuss various methods that work and what doesn't work in terms of freebies and giveaways. But get prepared to do the research and the work in creating something of value that you can giveaway in exchange for those all-important email addresses.

2. <u>Email Newsletter Content</u> – If you can entice people with the content on your site, then you can further entice them to sign-up to an email newsletter that will deliver fresh and valuable content to them periodically. You can promote the benefits of this as having never to check back to the site often and simply receiving the content directly to their inbox. But, you have to ensure that your offer and your site's content are compelling enough to drive this sign-up process home. Keep in mind that no one is going to sign-up to an email newsletter, or any email list for that matter, if they don't like the content that they're reading on the site. Of course, freebies and giveaways are a great way to entice people to offer

up their email addresses, but sometimes, merely offering access to a popular email list can be enough. However, getting to that point may take some time. Remember that this won't happen overnight. But, as long as you deliver content that's well-written, provides value, and is engaging, then you'll have no trouble in this area.

3. <u>Webinars</u> – Another way you can convert prospects into leads is by hosting Webinars. Webinars are Web-based seminars that allow you to hold a virtual meeting from anywhere in the world with any number of people. You can use several popular platforms for holding Webinars such as GoToMeeting.com or AnyMeeting.com, and you can even host a Hangout on Google Plus. Whatever type of virtual meeting you hold, you can use it to convert your prospects into leads as long as you have something of value to pitch. What are you selling? Why should they care? What type of valuable information are you going to want to offer? Make sure that you take the time to craft something that people are going to want. No matter what type of products, services, or information you're selling, you can create something of value in your niche or industry that will get people to stand up and take notice.

4. <u>Other Incentives</u> – You can offer other incentives in exchange for those trusted email addresses that could even involve offline marketing of services. For example, if you're already in business with a brick-and-mortar location, you could offer discounts, coupons, and freebies in-person in

exchange for those trusted email addresses. There are so many methods for obtaining email addresses, but you have to ensure that whatever method you do select, that it's an ethical method. Make sure you spend the time to brainstorm just what you can offer and make yourself a list. Run through the different options and see where you can promote your products, services, or information in exchange for those email addresses. You might just have to come up with some very enticing incentive if you don't plan to give something away online. Keep in mind that this is going to be critical to your long-term success on the Web because marketing is much more than just SEO; marketing involves weaving together so many different tasks and disciplines.

CONVERTING LEADS INTO SALES

Once you have your leads, this is where the delicate process of converting those leads into sales begins. This is where you have to put on your salesperson hat. You'll have to think and utilize certain strategies that will help to invoke a sale. Now, you'll have to ensure that all of your pieces to the online puzzle are in place first. You'll need some sort of product or service that you can sell on the Web, along with a purchasing process in place to sell them. Once you have that in place, you can aggressively conduct your sales campaigns by using a few different methods.

1. Email drip-campaigns – Email is going to be your biggest driver of sales. And the best part about it is that it can be automated. Now, you might be thinking that email marketing is dead but you'd be very wrong to assume so. Email-drip campaigns are one of the best semi-automated methods for

communicating with your leads and making sales. So what is it exactly and how is it different from a regular email? Well, email-drip campaigns require some configuration in the beginning but they are a semi-automated way to communicate with your customers. You can setup the emails that automatically will go out, not only when someone first signs up to your email newsletter, but also each email that will go out thereafter and the number of days between communications. This is an excellent way to communicate and use some proven selling techniques without having to craft new emails every day or every week.

2. <u>Email newsletter campaigns</u> – Email newsletter-campaigns differ from your email drip-campaigns in that email newsletter-campaigns are custom-crafted content that's also time-sensitive. You don't want to fully communicate with your leads only through drip-campaigns. You're also going to want to communicate fresh content that will help you provide value on a periodic basis without being too invasive. And, if you can continuously deliver on that value proposition, then you'll have those leads sticking around for a long time. If they can learn something new from you from time to time, then there's no reason why they won't remain loyal subscribers. But, this really does boil down to volume. As long as you have the volume in subscribers or leads, then you can effectively profit off email campaigns (both drip and newsletter content).

3. Product or service trials – One of the biggest and best methods for converting leads into sales, it also involves the most effort. In order to have an automated product or service trial on the Web, you have to put some serious work behind building up this trial or "freemium" system, so to speak. Now, this involves a much greater discussion than is within the scope of this book. However, it's important to keep these in mind at the outset, as you never know where the future can take you. Put your effort behind creating a system that will help to benefit your customers and allow them some time to take that system for a test-drive. Think about yourself for a moment and just how skeptical you are when it comes to trying out products and services that you're unsure of. No one wants to pay for a system that they potentially won't end up using. However, if you can give your leads a way to try that system out for free, then as long as they find value in it, they could end up becoming customers for a very long time.

2
MARKETING FUNDAMENTALS

In any discussion on Internet Marketing, it's important that we discuss the fundamentals. Now, you've learned about the fundamentals when it comes to SEO already in the first course entitled *SEO Fundamentals*. You also learned strategies and techniques for driving free organic search traffic to your site in the second course entitled, *SEO Strategies*. But, what you didn't learn are the specific marketing fundamentals for businesses on the Web. What do I mean by marketing fundamentals? Well, everyone knows that businesses on the Web that are found through Google on the first page of its SERPs are trusted listings. Because, when Google shows a particular listing at the top of its SERPs, which are all very competitive, it's clear that there's some trust behind that listing. But, we all know that getting on that coveted first page of is hard, no matter what you're selling or telling people.

So, what are we supposed to do? Well, we'll discuss some content marketing strategies by leveraging authority sites and that's going to be your best method for driving free organic traffic to your Website. But, first, you have to ensure that you have your sales funnel in place. So, how do we configure our sales funnel? Well, now that you've gone through with the optimization of your site, it's time to build that funnel. This is going to be the most important marketing piece that you have in place. Now, we briefly looked at just what a sales funnel is in the preceding chapter, but let's take a closer look. In essence, what we're doing is funneling visitors, which are prospects, into leads, and then into sales. So, as individuals make their way down the funnel, you're going to lose a large portion from stage to stage. Why is that? Well, it's the nature of marketing. What we need to do is leverage the volume of visitors and capitalize on them.

To build your first sales funnel you have to have a few key components in place. Without these components, you don't have a sales funnel. Now, whether you already have a Website and are conducting business on the Web or not, these components are going to be necessary. So, you'll have to do what's necessary in order to make some modifications to whatever system that you have in place right now in order to make things work properly. If you're already conducting business on the Web, or you've done so in the past, then you most likely have some system for generating leads. Most people simply leave a contact form, email address, or phone number on their Website for people to get in touch with them. Although this method is helpful, it isn't the proper way to conduct business on the Web from an Internet Marketing perspective. Why is that?

Well, you want to be able to entice people to provide their contact information to you, and not just the other way around. Sure, you want them to be able to get in touch, but it's more important that you be able to get in touch with them. To do this, you have to have the right components in place for generating those leads from the prospects. There has to be some incentive for them to give you their information. And, today, many people are skeptical to provide their contact information, even if it's just an email address, due to the prevalence of spam. People are sick of being promoted to repeatedly, so you have to ensure that when you do contact them, that you do so with tact. Put yourself in their shoes. Think about just how many spam messages you receive every single day and you'll realize why people are so reluctant to hand you their contact information. So, you have to create a compelling offer. You have to give the people a good enough reason to hand you their information. They're not just going to do it unwittingly.

So, let's look at the fundamentals involved with marketing on the Web. Here's a brief breakdown of the components involved:

1. <u>Website Optimized for SEO</u> – At the most basic layer of your marketing fundamentals is a Website optimized for SEO. If you haven't properly addressed your site for optimization, then now is the time to do so. Ensure that things like your CSS structure is clean, keywords are properly researched, and that your Website's static pages are optimized for a primary keyword. So, if you're in the business of "Resume Writing Services," then your Website's static pages should be optimized for that primary keyword.

2. <u>Content Optimized for SEO</u> – When content is optimized for SEO, it helps to drive traffic on a consistent basis. This runs in conjunction with a Website that's optimized for SEO, but content-

optimization focuses on a variety of keywords whereas the Website optimization focuses on a primary keyword target. Content optimization is an ongoing task whereas Website's static page-content optimization is something that's primarily done one time.

3. <u>Sales Funnel with Opt-In Incentive</u> – Beyond the static and fresh content, is your sales funnel. Now, content is a precursor to your sales funnel since it will help to ultimately drive traffic to your site and keep it there. But the sales funnel is what'll bring people closer to the hip with you, so to speak. When prospects land on your site, they will start to review your content. They'll read static and fresh content through your blog and site's pages. If they like what they see, they might just opt-in to receive more communications from your on a regular basis. This is when they'll drop into your sales funnel.

4. <u>Email-Based Campaigns</u> – Marketing the right way includes communicating the right way via email. You must know how to communicate, as in what type of language to use, and how often to communicate. No one likes to receive constant communication over and over again from someone always trying to sell their products or services. You have to use tact, provide value in your communications, and allow the selling to happen on autopilot. This is one of the fundamental necessities of running an online business. No matter what you're selling – products, services, or information – doing that on

autopilot through email-based campaigns will help to free up your time to focus on other areas of importance.

5. <u>Purchase, Review, And Refer</u> – The purchase process is the crowning achievement in selling anything on the Web. We all want to get consumers to purchase whatever it is that we're peddling. But, you shouldn't focus solely on the purchase at the expense of everything else. While getting someone to purchase something from you might feel empowering, ensuring that what they're purchasing from you is 100% quality through-and-through is paramount. You want that purchaser to then be able to review whatever it is that you sold them. If it was a service, you want them to tout that service to friends, family, and followers anywhere and everywhere. So, a fundamental part of marketing has to do with online reviews. Find a place where customers can leave you reviews for what you sold them. Whether it's on Yelp, TripAdvisor, Angie's List, or some other trusted online resource, ensure that you communicate this with them. Once they've reviewed, you want to give them a way they can refer people to you. This will be the best kind of business: word-of-mouth.

WEBSITE OPTIMIZED FOR SEO

The first component in the marketing fundamentals for any business on the Web is site-wide optimization for SEO. As you may already know, optimizing a Website site-wide for SEO involves some fundamental rules and principles that were already covered in the first course of the SEO University entitled, *SEO Fundamentals*. When it comes to site-wide optimization, some key factors must be addressed, which are as follows:

- **Design and Content Guidelines** – Google's design and content guidelines relate to the overall appearance of the site itself and to its functionality. These are aesthetic guidelines but they also include functional ones as well. Most of these guidelines are the basis for the Google Panda algorithm update, and it's important that you adhere to them. Google is merely trying to ensure a rich user-experience, allowing a visitor to your site to easily navigate around and find what he or she is looking for quickly.

- Site hierarchy and text links – Google wants to ensure that the Website has a clear hierarchy and is easy navigable. You must be able to get to any point in the site from any of the other static pages. When designing a site, it's important to keep the site hierarchy in mind. If the site is a blog, then ensure that the menu items allow a user to easily navigate between the sections of the blog to quickly find the information that they're looking for.

- Offer a site map to users – A site map is critical for Google and users. It wants to ensure that not only a search engine will be able to find what it's looking for quickly, but also users as well. In fact, it's more concerned with how easily users are able to navigate a site than a search engine is. Create a site map, and if there are many pages, break the site map out into multiple pages.

- Reasonable number of links – This rule is both an aesthetic one and a functional one as well. Any time there's an overcrowding of outbound links, Google is sure to take notice. This is especially true when the content is very thin. But, regardless of just how much content is on the page, never overcrowd the page with too many links out to other sites. This was something common in the content and link-farming days, which were the targets of the Google Panda and Google Penguin algorithm updates. Keep the outbound links to a minimum and the content to a very high standard.

- Information-rich content – Google wants to ensure that the content you're providing is information-rich. What does this mean? Well, as previously stated, you must be adding a great deal of value, and it must be unique and engaging. Spend the time to write well-researched articles that help answer questions in the most proficient and well thought out ways possible. Never skimp on providing information-rich content. Always think value. Always.

- Keyword-driven content – Google wants to ensure that the Webpage has a purpose, and that the purpose is keyword-driven. Google wants to be able to understand just what the page is about. When the page has no general purpose, Google loses interest and the page loses rank. And, if you're writing a Webpage or article about one particular question or topic, don't veer far off that topic. Stay on the topic and ensure that all of the information and content is relevant to that topic. Don't try to clutter the

Webpage with excessive keywords that don't properly pertain to the overall topic of the page.

- Text links as opposed to images – Google can't read images; at least not today, it can't. So, it wants you to use text links as opposed to images wherever possible. Years ago, it was much more difficult to make text appear and aligned like images. But today, with the use of CSS, all that has changed. Try to keep to an all-text and CSS approach if you can, and keep the graphics to a bare minimum while focusing on the content instead. And, when images are used, make sure that they are properly labeled with Image <ALT> tags so that Google can distinguish their purpose.

- Usage of <TITLE> and <ALT> attributes – The <TITLE> tag relates to the Website's header, and it provides the descriptive outline for what the page is about. The <TITLE> tag is also the same tag that's used by Google to provide the title of your page on its SERPs. Ensure that you properly utilize the <TITLE> tag of your page by placing the keyword-rich title there that accurately depicts what the page is about. And, again, when using images on your Webpage, always ensure that <ALT> attributes are used to describe them. Usage of the page's primary keyword in an <ALT> tag is also highly recommended.

- Check for broken links – No one likes broken links, especially Google. If you're creating a Webpage, no matter what it's about, always go back and ensure the accuracy of the links. Do all of the links work? Do all of the links point to valid pages on the Internet? If not, go back and fix them. Google will check your pages for accuracy in broken links. Always ensure that you have a 100% working-links ratio to not lose the potential for ranking.

- URL rules for dynamic pages – Whether you're familiar with dynamic pages or not, it's important to keep in mind that Google wants to find the primary keyword in the page's URL, or something that's semantically similar to it. Furthermore, when using Web programming such as PHP, more than one variable after the URL won't be indexed. Keep the parameters short if you must have them in the URL, since static pages are crawled much more efficiently than dynamic ones are.

- Image rules – Google can't read images. It can't decipher text inside images or other relevant information; or at least not at this moment in time. For that reason, you have to be as descriptive as possible with your images. Rather than using a name like IMG12345.jpg, try to name the image with the primary keyword of the page. If the page is about "iPhone 7 Rumors," give the main image a title like iphone-7-rumors-graphic.jpg. This is much more descriptive and informative than a random image name. Furthermore, use the image <ALT> attribute to add further clarification with the keyword. But, don't attempt to stuff keywords into the image <ALT> attribute, as it will only hurt you as opposed to helping you.

- Image quality – Remember to always keep in mind that Google wants browsers to have a rich user-experience. Ensure that the quality of your photos is high and that they relevantly pertain to the context of the Webpage that they're on. Google is much more likely to like a page with high-quality photos than one with low-quality photos. Stay away from using blurry or obscure photos that don't pertain to the content. Furthermore, stay away from poaching other images from Websites where possible. Try to keep your content and your images as original as possible. If you must use images found on other sites, be sure to properly credit and name your sources.

- Image Dimensions – Make sure that you always provide a height and a width in pixels for your images. This is achieved by using the height and width attributes within the image tag itself.

- Image Location – Google knows that most users will not scroll to the bottom of the Webpage, so it's important to keep your primary image for the Webpage as close to the top as possible.

  o Video rules – Google is constantly improving its search algorithms to encompass a wide variety of searchable data, which includes videos. Videos are a great way to help increase the relevance of a Webpage, but they also must be properly presented and identified to the Google search engine. Google recommends using schema.org for marking up video information on a site.

- **Technical Guidelines** – These guidelines relate more to the technical aspects – namely the coding – of a site or Webpage. These guidelines are important because Google places some weight on the browsability, discoverability, and overall cross-browser experience of any given Webpage. If it feels like a Webpage falls short, so will its rankings. If you're not in-the-know from a coding standpoint, then it's important to find a professional who can help assist in this area.

- Limit usage of JavaScript, Flash, and DHTML – In an effort to keep load time and cross-browser compatibility at efficient levels, Google discourages the usage of Flash, JavaScript, and DHTML. For the most part, all of this can be achieved today with dynamic HTML markup and CSS, so it's best that you stay away from anything that's going to slow the load time of a Webpage.

- Handling Session IDs – Session IDs are used very commonly to track the behavior of visitors to sites. These could include things like Website Cookies and Login Sessions. If your site is using sessions, ensure that WebCrawlers will be able to still access the pertinent pages on the site for indexing purposes. It's important that a search engine spider such as Google's be able to crawl without the usage of sessions.

- HTTP Header support – It's important to ensure that the web server that you're using supports the If-Modified-Since HTTP Header. This allows Google to know whether a Webpage was updated since it last visited the page. This will save bandwidth and overhead in the instance where information was not updated on a particular page since the WebCrawler's last visit.

- Using robots.txt – This is going to be an important part of the process in SEO. You must ensure that you generate a robots.txt so that unintended pages aren't crawled. You can use robots.txt to tell search engine spiders like Google's to only crawl certain pages or directories.

- Over-usage of ads – Google doesn't want to see a high ad-to-content ratio. Rather, it wants it to be the other way around. Make sure that your page isn't filled with too many ads. Even if you have many high-quality posts, limit the ads to a reasonable number. Google knows that no user wants to sift through endless amounts of ads, even if the ads are non-invasive and off to the side of the Webpage.

- Crawlable pages with CMS systems – If you're using a CMS system to create your Webpages, it's important that the pages be crawlable. Some CMS systems will create pages and links that search engines can't crawl. Always ensure that all of your pages are properly crawlable and accessible to search engines for the highest-quality browsing experience possible.

- o Cross-browser compatibility – Whether it's Internet Explorer, Safari, Firefox, Chrome, or any other browser, always ensure that your pages properly appear across all platforms. You could easily lose search rankings based on Google's algorithms if your pages don't look and behave consistently across browsers. Test and re-test using popular available tools for cross-browser compatibility checks. If you're using Wordpress or other blogging platforms, you'll have less to worry about unless you've created a custom theme.

- o Optimization of load-times – Don't overload your pages with heavy and slow-loading graphics. This should already be clear to you as it diminishes the user's browser experience. Just imagine yourself when you have to sit through and wait for a slow-loading site to finally load all of its components. Keep the images to a minimum level.

- **Quality Guidelines** – The quality guidelines of a Website have as much to do with Black-Hat SEO as they do with White-Hat SEO. You must adhere to these basic principles and specific practices in order to stay in Google's good graces. By now, you should understand that Google is looking for high-quality content that's engaging and provides value. But you must pay attention to all the other details of aesthetics and functionality as well.

- **Basic Principles**
    - Pages designed for users not search engines
    - Avoiding deception
    - Avoiding search-engine-optimization tricks
    - Creating unique content that's engaging and adds value

- **Specific Practices**
    - Avoid automatically generated content
    - Don't participate in link schemes
    - Don't engage in content cloaking
    - Don't engage in sneaky redirects
    - Don't hide text or links
    - Don't create doorway pages
    - Don't scrape content
    - Don't participate in affiliate programs without adding a lot of value
    - Don't add irrelevant keywords

- Don't create pages with malicious behavior (i.e. phishing, Trojans, malware, viruses, etc.)
- Don't abuse rich-snippet markup
- Don't send automated queries to Google
- Monitor your site for hacking
- Prevent and remove user-generated spam from your site

CONTENT OPTIMIZED FOR SEO

Beyond the technical, design, and quality guidelines that are applicable site-wide, there are the marketing fundamental rules as they relate to content. Of course, you have to ensure that your content is optimized for SEO. If it weren't, it would defeat the entire purpose of marketing a business on the Web. Even if you're running paid marketing, the content has to be well-written and optimized for your keywords, whatever those keywords may be, as this helps to build organic rank over time. Although we addressed content optimization for SEO in the first course of the SEO University, *SEO Fundamentals*, here's a brief summary of that information:

- Content Length – The content length should be at least 500 to 1000 words in length. Want to go a step further? Today, excellent content over 1000 words in length seems to actually rank best.

Ensure that when you're creating your high-quality content that none of it sounds spammy, forced, or has spelling and grammatical errors. All of these would bring the quality of the content down in Google's eyes, and thus the relevancy. So, do your best to ensure that it looks and sounds as perfect as possible.

- <u>Keyword Density</u> – The keyword density relates to the number of times a keyword appears versus the total number of words in the article. Now, this keyword density is going to be calculated by both the primary keyword and the secondary keywords that include LSI variations of the primary keyword. If you'll recall, LSI keywords are something we discussed in previous courses. So, the optimal keyword density that you're looking to reach should be 2% to 5% so you'll want to have 2 to 5 keywords for every 100 words of your article. So, if you have a 500-word article, then the optimal keyword length is going to be 10 to 25 keywords. And, for a 1000-word article, it's going to be 20 to 50 keywords.

- <u>Keyword in URL</u> – Ensure that the page title contains the primary keyword or an LSI version of it. You can turn on page titles in Wordpress by going to Settings > Permalinks > Post name. This will use the Wordpress title to generate a page name, which can then be edited before or after publication. Remember the discussion about image names and how Google wants a relevant name to the image? Well, the same rule applies to the page name itself. The more specific the title, and the more it applies to the overall primary keyword of the content, the better.

- <u>Keyword in Title</u> – Use the primary keyword or an LSI version of it in the page's title, which is generally considered the <H1> tag. You should also use the keyword in at least one <H2> tag and <H3> tag. Furthermore, you should section off your article or post so that it's not just one long piece of content. Google wants content that's easy to read and digestible, and section headings assist in that. Ensure that you break up your article into multiple sections, and use the primary keyword and LSI versions of it in those headings.

- <u>Keywords in Content</u> – Ensure that you use your primary keyword or an LSI variation of it at least once in the first paragraph and once in the last paragraph of the content. Google places special weight on these sections of the content as it further clarifies that this piece of content is about is about your primary keyword. You should also distribute the remainder of your keywords throughout the balance of your content, but ensure that it never sounds forced. Spammy content that just attempts to use a maximum amount of keywords will not win points with Google. Google will consider this keyword stuffing.

- <u>Keyword Styling</u> – Ensure that you style your primary keyword or the LSI variations of it. This means that you should use your keyword at least once in boldface font, once in italics, and once in underlined font. Again, this helps to further clarify and target this piece of content to that keyword. Make sure to distribute your stylized texts throughout the content of the Webpage and don't place them all in one section or paragraph. Overall, try to achieve a good balance of keywords throughout the article, without flooding one particular paragraph or section of it.

- Keyword in Meta Description – If you're unfamiliar with a Webpage's Meta description, now's the time to familiarize yourself with it. The page's title is the title tag that you'll see on Google searches when you obtain search results, and the description will actually come from the Meta description. Now, if the page doesn't have a Meta description, then Google will find a paragraph that will best describe the content itself. But, it's best to go out there and create your own Meta description. By default, you currently cannot create a unique Meta description for each article posted on Wordpress blogs. But, you can download a plugin such as the Yoast SEO Plugin in order to modify the Meta description per article posted on your Wordpress blog.

- Keywords in Images – You have at least one high-quality photo on your blog and you should name it with your keyword or an LSI variation of it. Furthermore, when you upload your photo, you should add an ALT tag with your keyword or the LSI variation of it. This will solidify the purpose of the Webpage or article, since the image will drive home the fact that this is a keyword-driven page and just what that keyword is.

On-Page Optimization

1. Use the primary keyword once in page title <H1> tag, once in an <H2> tag and once in an <H3> tag

2. Use the primary keyword in the first paragraph and in the last paragraph

3. Use the primary keyword in the image ALT tag for the Webpage

4. Use the primary keyword **once in bold font**, once *in italics font*, and once in underlined font

5. Use a primary keyword density of 2% to 5% that sounds natural and flows organically

6. Use the primary keyword in the Webpage or article's meta description

7. Make sure primary keyword shows up in the page title, if you are using Wordpress, turn on permalinks and use the "postname" option

SALES FUNNEL WITH OPT-IN INCENTIVE

While the first two points were addressed in prior courses, what we didn't address before, which we'll be addressing now in detail, is the sales funnel. This is going to be the most important part of your Website. It's going to be the driving-force behind your sales. In fact, it's going to be the engine or drive-train of the vehicle that will be called your Website. Because, the sales funnel is going to be at the very heart of your business. It's going to be the heartbeat that will make things tick. Without a proper sales funnel, there would be virtually no point in having a business on the Web, especially if that business involves the desire to profit in one way or another. Now, that profit shouldn't be at the expense of other things. If you have a passion for what you're doing, you shouldn't skimp on the value-proposition of your content, products, services, or information solely in a desire for economic enhancement.

The sales funnel is merely there to facilitate

transactions and slowly filter prospects down through the various stages that ultimately lead to a sale. The better your sales funnel is, the more likely you're going to be to profit from your traffic. If your sales funnel is flimsy, then you can't expect great returns from your hard work. So, building a solid sales funnel is going to take center stage when it comes to *SEO for Business*. Yes, we want to drive traffic to the site, but we also want to capitalize on that traffic. If we're not capitalizing on the traffic, we're wasting our time. So, how are we going to build that sales funnel? What are we going to give away that's going to entice people just enough to hand over their basic information? Are they going to trust you, your site, or your content when they arrive at your virtual storefront? Or, are they going to quickly jump off the page just as fast as they landed there?

Well, just how good you are at executing your sales funnel is going to be equivalent to your success in business on the Web. Even if you're devoted to building sites for clients, effective sales funnel construction is a skill that you can use to build numerous niche businesses on the Web. Niche Websites, as I'm sure you've heard already, are used by some of the top online marketers to generate tremendous amounts of passive income. But we all have to start somewhere. So, what does it take to put the sales funnel in place? Well, let's look at just how prospects are lured into your funnel. Once they're at your Website, funneling them into your sales and marketing engine is going to take some convincing. You'll need to have some excellent content that will build trust with the prospects first. But considering that you have all of that in place, here's how you'll get them to drop into your sales funnel, which you saw me allude to earlier on in the preceding chapter.

1. Freebies & Giveaways
2. Email Newsletter Content
3. Webinars
4. Other Incentives

But in order to establish this funnel you'll need a system for collecting email addresses. And that system will have to be incorporated into your Website. You've seen this before, probably hundreds or even thousands of times. Off to the right side of the screen, or even through some pop-up on the site itself, you'll have the offer that would include the entry of the email address. And in order to integrate that email capture into your Website, you'll need to use one of the systems available on the Web, which would allow you to integrate an email capture system. There are three widely used systems for doing so:

1. GetResponse.com
2. AWeber.com
3. ConstantContact.com

Regardless of what system you use, you'll be able to integrate and manage an email capture onto your Website with each system. Then, you'll be able to build out an email newsletter with an email-drip campaign that will automatically communicate with your leads. But, we'll get to this later. For now, you'll have to ensure that you have something you want to giveaway in place of that prospect offering up their email address to you. What kind of offer are you going to give away? Will it be a free ebook? Will it be a free online tutorial or video to help them do something? Or, maybe you'll conduct a Webinar that will help them to realize the importance of whatever it is you're selling. Or, maybe you want to promote the fact that you have an incredible newsletter with dazzling content that goes out every week. Whatever it is, you have to decide and take action. This is going to be integral to your sales funnel.

EMAIL-BASED CAMPAIGNS

Once you have your leads in your system, marketing fundamentals don't end there. Just because you were able to convince a prospect to become a lead by giving you their email address, it doesn't mean that the hard work is done or that you can abuse that trust. You have to operate on a certain set of principles when communicating with your leads. And it's during that communication that trust can either be built up or destroyed. You can't over-communicate with your leads, especially when that communication comes across as spammy or trying to over-sell. And, you can't under-communicate with your leads as well, allowing them to forget about you. You have to walk that fine line of providing valuable communications that will help to enhance peoples' lives, but not overdoing it. Selling should be more of a by-product than your primary objective.

So how are you supposed to make any money? How are you supposed to build an effective sales funnel if you can't market frequently? Well, that's because your focus must be on providing value. Even if you're trying to promote your business, it should be a by-product to your desire to provide value. That's the way that you'll be able to constantly crank profits on a consistent basis. When you build your email-based campaigns, they should communicate periodically and focus on the desire to provide value. For example, if you send out 6 emails per month – one every 5 days – two-thirds of those emails should be focused on providing value and not selling. Selling can be a by-product of those emails, but the focus should be on value. This means that you should be providing important industry information, how-to articles, video tutorials, and anything else that might help to provide value. When you focus on value and you don't over promote your business, you will earn the trust of your subscriber base.

When you don't focus on providing value, and you don't over promote, you also won't lose your subscriber base. Remember, they can and will unsubscribe from your email list if you violate their trust. We'll get into more of the specifics of what it takes to effectively communicate with your subscriber base, but for now, it's important to understand that you have to earn and build the trust of your subscribers. If there's something that you think that might violate their trust, such as selling off their information to other providers, don't do it. Keep things aboveboard at all times, and in the long run, you'll build trust and your business. So, what do we need to do in order to communicate properly? Well, here are some basic rules to the fundamentals when communicating via email with your subscriber base:

1. **Don't over-communicate** – This is where you have to walk a fine line in communication. Once you have that email address, your email-drip campaigns and one-off emails should only communicate with them every few days. Definitely not every day; and absolutely not multiple times each day. Remember, email communication is a sacred thing that can easily be abused.

2. **Don't under-communicate** – You don't want your subscribers to forget about you. So, make sure you communicate at least once a week or once every other week. If you're slowly getting into email marketing, then you can ease yourself into it like this. But, don't go months without communicating. Every now and then, drop your subscribers a message and share some valuable information or offer with them.

3. **Sell less than two-thirds of the time** – For every 10 emails you send, 6 or so emails should be value-based, and the other 3 or 4 should be promotional-based. No matter what you've read about email marketing, absolutely do not try to sell on every message that you send out. It's annoying to people. They want to learn something interesting from you. Present yourself as an authority and teach your subscribers something they might not have known. Remember: make your selling almost a by-product.

4. **Make your emails personal** – Your emails should be personal. Don't try to sound too corporate or come off like a huge company if you're not. People like to connect on a real and emotional level. Share something of value, but do it in a personal way. You can even throw in a personal photo or detail every now and then. But tread with caution and with care. Use tact. To make things more personal, you could even use the "P.S." moniker at the end, or even "P.P.S." to add extra points. This gives a much more personal touch.

5. **Always have a call to action** – Each email should have a call to action. For example, even if you're sharing something of value, your email should be brief. Maybe you just wrote a great blog article on your site that you want to share with them. Place two or three calls to action within that email directing them to click on the link to read more about your article. Maybe you share the first few juicy points of your article, and direct them to your site for the rest. This doesn't mean you should sell something in your emails. Just have a call to action. You always want to engage your subscribers to do something in your emails.

6. **Write copy that delivers value** – Again, here's that principle that we've seen over and over again: value. You absolutely must deliver value in everything that you produce, whether it's offline or online. And, especially when it comes to sending emails to subscribers, those messages must contain valuable information. For example,

if you're selling resume-writing services, why not offer the top 10 tips for preparing the perfect resume? Or, the top 7 biggest mistakes made in interviews? Get the point? Offer something of value in your emails.

7. **Write clickable subject lines** – This is an art form. If you're not a writer, you absolutely must get good at this. Every marketer must understand how to write subject lines that are clickable, and create content that provides value, and ultimately drives sales. Take a writing course at your local college, or find some online courses. But, overall, here are some key pointers on writing clickable subject lines:

   a. **Be descriptive & informative** – The subject-line of the email should convey its purpose in a strong and compelling manner that highlights the immediate benefit to the reader. Don't try to be too artsy with your subject-lines. Use straightforward, descriptive subject-lines that clearly describe the content you're sending.

   b. **Use lists where possible** – People enjoy reading lists. Make your subject line a "Top 10" list, or "Top 12" list, or anything else that sounds catchy. And, come up with genuine and unique content that provides value. This can be a positive list, or a negative one. For example, "Top 10 Ways to Improve your Marriage", or, "7 Ways to Avoid Ruining your Marriage."

c. **Use question-driven titles** – Another great method for sending emails with clickable subject-lines, is to use question-driven titles. For example, "How Do I Avoid Losing My Job," or "What are the Best Ways to Market My Business," and "When Is the Best Time to Sell Your Home?" Get the picture? These question-driven titles should spur people to click, and also provide value to them. Write about something in your niche that you think people would appreciate.

8. **Track and analyze statistics** – You won't know if your marketing efforts are paying off if you don't track and analyze your statistics. You'll want to know things like the email-open rate, or click-through ratios, and so on. The email providers provide these statistics. Companies like GetResponse.com, AWeber.com, and ConstantContact.com provide excellent tracking and analysis tools. This helps to determine things like: when the best time to send your emails are, or which emails got the most spam complaints, and so on. As an online marketer, you must meticulously track everything.

PURCHASE, REVIEW, REFER

So much of our online behavior has to do with the reading and writing of reviews that's it's become central in our lives. When we look to purchase something on the Web, we do a quick search to glean what others have experienced who have done the same. That's why focusing on value from the very beginning is so important. The same fundamentals that apply to building PageRank through SEO over time with your optimization efforts, also apply to your business. You have to ensure that whatever it is you're selling is of greater value than the money being exchanged for it. In fact, this is a fundamental law in successful businesses. You simply cannot go out there with a subpar product and expect to do well over time because people are going to talk. And, when people talk, you had better believe that other people are going to listen.

Knowing all of this, and knowing that you're going to ultimately make sales on the Web, you really have to focus your efforts on providing an excellent product or service. No matter what you're selling, it has to be a cut above the rest. You have to go that extra mile because that's how great businesses are built. I know that this isn't a course on economics, customer service, or even the creation of a business itself, but these fundamentals have to hold true for you. And, you also have to facilitate a way for customers to leave you feedback somewhere on the Web. Why is this important? Well, knowing that customers are going to talk, you have to give them an outlet to do so. If you're in a travel-related business, you can use a site like TripAdvisor. Or, if you're in a physical business, you can use a site like Yelp.com. And, no matter what business you're in, you can use a slew of other sites such as:

1. AngiesList.com
2. Google Plus/Local/Places
3. Yahoo Local
4. InsiderPages.com
5. CitySearch.com
6. ConsumerSearch.com
7. BBB.org
8. Facebook.com
9. LinkedIn.com
10. Twitter.com

Of course, you can also setup a review system on your

own Website, but most people will be more wary of that since you have full control. Even on social media sites, where you get to control the content on your pages, reviews may be less trusted. However, by petitioning customers to leave reviews on something like your Facebook Fan or Business Page, you can certainly build up some trust. But, no matter where you direct customers, you have to set this up beforehand so that you have some place to send customers that want to leave reviews. They are going to find places to leave you reviews anyhow, especially if they were dissatisfied with some product or service that you offered. So, give them an outlet from the beginning. It will show more trust and show that you're committed to their satisfaction. This can help bolster sales for just about any business. When customers see that a business is proudly displaying their online reviews from some trusted source, they are much more likely to do business with that company.

Furthermore, one of the most important parts of the process is to allow customers the opportunity to refer you. So, how is this done? Well, there are several ways that you can allow them to do this, but most importantly, you'll need a refer-a-friend function located somewhere. Now, you can entice them to refer you by giving them a voucher for credit towards free products or services with you. Or, you can merely provide a link that will allow them to refer you. However, you'll need to setup a system that allows you to track just who referred you a client. This can be done through an affiliate system, or through online software that's available, which can assist you with customer referrals.

3
LOCAL SEO

Beyond the fundamental aspects of marketing of the Web, along with the basics of SEO, comes the more specialized field of local SEO. This is where we'll be turning our attention to the niche marketplace in an effort to boost awareness, traffic, and sales for a business. This truly is the heart of *SEO for Business*. But it doesn't just happen with local SEO alone. This requires a multi-pronged approach that also includes content marketing, sales funnels, and email marketing. The combination of all of these elements together helps to drive traffic, create leads, and produce sales without having to wait forever.

Local SEO helps to bridge that divide that comes anytime you try to build the organic search rankings of a business that's relatively new. When the site is relatively new, it lacks Google's trust, something that we've already covered exhaustively in the prior two courses. But, building trust for a local business is far easier than building it for, say, just a blog that has no direct sales interaction between its owner and its visitors. With your local business, your strategy really is going to be to get out there to all the important outlets before you engage in any crafty content marketing.

So, how does this work? Well, the goal here is to leverage existing services that will allow you to build trust directly for your business listing through outlets like Google Plus, Yelp, Facebook, and LinkedIn. We want to build authority through these sites, but we want to do it in a specific way. You see, all of these sites leverage online reviews to help vet businesses through the local community. The focus, then, is not only SEO that's localized, but also reviews to help build that trust. But, the way in which your business listing is added to these sites is also important.

For example, let's just say that you provide cleaning services in New York City. You run a service that cleans short-term rental apartments in Downtown Manhattan. Let's also say that your business is called John's Cleaning, Inc. Now, what most people would do is to add their business name exactly as it appears to all of the online sites, which is not the best approach if you're trying to be highly-targeted. So, how do you do it? Well, rather than creating a Google Plus page for John's Cleaning, Inc., let's look at how we would spin the name of that listing so that we can better target it from a local SEO perspective.

So, how would you do it if you were put to the task? First, you would have to understand your target audience. If you did the work and you covered the material presented in the prior two courses, then you most likely have a solid handle on that. If you didn't, now is the time to go and review that material. If you'll recall our discussion about long-tail keywords, this is where you'll have to get creative about your company's public name. The more keyword-rich you make the name of your business on public listings, the better it will be for the business. So, if you're running a cleaning service in Downtown Manhattan, have you done the research to see just what terms people are using to find businesses like yours?

Regardless, if you run a cleaning service, an accounting firm, or any other type of business, you must know, not only your target consumer, but also your target search. When you've understood this, and you've used the Google Keyword Planner as discussed in prior courses, then you should have come up with some long-tail keywords that help to target what you're offering. So, instead of writing John's Cleaning, Inc., you could use something like:

1. Apartment Cleaning Service Downtown Manhattan
2. Best Lower Manhattan Cleaning Company
3. Downtown Manhattan Apartment Cleaning Crew

Now, the goal here is to stay consistent with the name of your business. Using a keyword in one listing, then changing the keywords in another is going to confuse people. If someone is searching for information on your company, you should also put the real name of the company within the description itself. But, this localized SEO is important, especially when posting this information on business sites that will provide local listings such as Google Plus so that your listing shows up in Google Maps, on Yelp, Foursquare, SuperPages, and every other place on the Web.

BUSINESS LISTINGS

Your keyword-rich business listing title that you've now researched using Google's Keyword Planner must also tie in well with the fundamental optimization of your site. If you've spent little time optimizing your business's Website for keywords, then now is the time to do so. When conducting local SEO, it's simply not enough to just use long-tail keywords that are keyword-rich for your targeted niche or business's consumer. You also have to optimize your site for those targeted keywords. If you don't have a blog using a system like Wordpress, then this goal is going to be more difficult to achieve.

However, I'm going to assume that you did the work from the past two courses, that you have a system in place for releasing fresh content, and that you've done some work in optimizing your site for keywords that are targeting your business, niche, or customer demographic. Now, the task is to craft a long-tail keyword that's highly specific, which can be used in your online profiles and business listings. You're going to use this as your business name for these profile listings. Why use it as your business name? Well, as we've seen from the past two courses, titles of pages on any type of site hold particular sway in SEO. In fact, Google generally derives its listings on its SERPs from page titles.

So, you have to create a title that's going to be highly specific. Now, I can't tell you what that title is going to be; you'll need to do the research using the Google Keyword Planner Tool, as previously discussed in the past two courses. But, I will offer you some guidelines to help you along the way. What you need to think about here are the factors that influence your search. This goes a little bit beyond optimizing for articles or posts on your site, since this has to be a macro-targeted keyword. You're looking for something that will help to describe your whole business, product, or service in long-form. This is going to vary from person to person, or business to business.

Everyone's business is relatively unique – this much is obvious. Regardless, if they sell the same things, people like to add their own spin to their business. Your goal must be to find something that will not only help to describe you in the local-search sense with maximum exposure, but also something that will set you apart as well. There also must be a heavy focus on customer reviews, because customer reviews and reputation is the new currency of the digital age. The more trusted you are, the quicker you're going get traction moving forward.

So, where do we begin?

First, let's look at the sites we'll be using to post your listings. These sites will help you build the most local authority in the quickest manner. Think about this. When you search for a local business on Google, what do you look for? You most likely enter in some keywords that will help to best describe what you're going after. If you're looking for a new hairdresser, you might say, "Best haircut in Nassau County," or "Best men's haircut in Miami Beach," or "Best hair salons for women in Pasadena." You get the picture, right?

You want to describe your business how a person would be searching for it. Now, you might not want to go out on a limb and describe your business as the best of doing something, especially if you're just getting started. But, that doesn't mean you can't come up with other clever ways to name your listing, in hopes of targeting a specific keyword search. If you did the work and analyzed some search keywords using the Google Keyword Planner, you should have a good idea of some long-tail keywords that would best apply to your overall business.

Now, in order to post those listings, you'll need some profiles setup on popular sites. Here's what we want to target:

- **Google Local Business Listings** - http://www.google.com/business - This will allow you to show up on Google Maps for your local area, town, city, county, or even state. Depending upon how you post this listing, and how well-received it is in the form of reviews, this can provide a tremendous boost in overall rankings. Plus, this adds another authority link coming to your site.

- **Google Plus Business Page** - https://plus.google.com/pages/create - Another great resource to help increase exposure for your business is also Google Plus for Business. In essence, you'll be creating a business page for your business on Google Plus. This business page will also be keyword-rich and have a powerful and high PageRank backlink to your site. This will also be a great resource for garnering online reviews for your business as well.

- **Facebook Business Page** - https://www.facebook.com/business/overview - Of course, what more important resource could you use to drive traffic to your business, than a Facebook Page? Setup a business page that will not only help to drive traffic to your business, but will also build on that high PageRank link source. Keep in mind that you'll also be able to garner reviews through Facebook for your business.

- **Yelp for Business** - https://biz.yelp.com - Yelp is quite possibly one of the most important resources you can list your business. And, considering the high PageRank, an inbound link from Yelp can help to boost your site's awareness tremendously. You can also use it to respond to reviews as the owner of the business, measure what a visitor does when they view your listing, and convert those visitors into customers.

- **Bing Business Listing** - https://www.bingplaces.com - Yes, it's not Google, but Bing is still an important resource on the Web, with an even more important high

PageRank backlink coming to your site. Be sure to setup a business listing on Bing so that you can be found across all of its services, which include maps, on the Web, and mobile.

- **SuperPages** — http://www.superpages.com/about/new_chg_listing.html -SuperPages are the Yellow Pages of the Internet. Back in the day, we all used to receive a big, thick, yellow booklet that would outline all the businesses in our area. Those days are long gone now. Today, the Yellow Pages reside on the Internet, but SuperPages is another excellent resource for traffic and high PageRank link-source.

- **Yahoo Business Listings** — https://smallbusiness.yahoo.com/local-listings - There was a time, not that long ago, when Yahoo was the ruler of the Web. Until of course, Google came around. But, Yahoo is still one of the most important resources for traffic through content, even if they no longer are the primary provider of a search engine. Listing your business on Yahoo is just another way to drive traffic to your business and provide another high PageRank link source.

- **Foursquare** - http://business.foursquare.com/claim - Another very popular map-based resource for you to list your business, Foursquare allows you to tie into that social element that has evolved. On

Foursquare, customers are able to leave tips and photos about businesses, letting other people know just what they love the most about each place. You can use Foursquare to tap into that local element, and increase your exposure.

- **Yext** - http://www.yext.com/customers/smallbusiness - The last resource that wanted to talk about is Yext. In fact, a Yext PowerListing is a very intuitive way to go about listing your business on some of the most important sites on the Web. They'll work to synchronize your information across all of these listings, and more. They target a network of 50+ leading Websites, maps, and applications. However, it's important to note that Yext PowerListings aren't free. If you don't have the time to do the work, but you do have the extra money to spare, you might want to consider it. Otherwise, you'll have to pound away at that trusty keyboard yourself.

ONLINE REVIEWS

One thing most people forget about, when starting out with their business from an SEO standpoint, are online reviews. Now, there are some very important points that I want to make here about online reviews. The first point is that Google has recently begun to calibrate and tweak some of its local search algorithms to include reviews from trusted resources. Now, I wouldn't bet the farm on throwing all your focus into your reviews, but you should be very aware of them.

I'll also say here that you should absolutely be honest with your reviews. If you run a real business, or you intend to run a real business, then you should solicit every single customer or client to post a review about your work. If you work with people on the phone, tell them upfront that you're dedicated to their satisfaction, and that you'd like them to post a review on the Web about their experience when it's all over.

But this isn't just about getting good reviews; this is also about avoiding bad reviews. Why is that? Well, in 2010, the New York Times ran a big feature about a sunglass merchant called Décor My Eyes. They detailed how the owner was convinced that people complaining about him on the Web would actually increase his online presence, helping him to rank better. Those links to his site would allow him to build authority.

That would be the general consensus, wouldn't it? Even if people were complaining on the Web, with inbound links to a site, you would think that it would increase in PageRank, right? Well, it did for a while. But that's all changed now. Google instituted some dramatic changes that saw poor reviews actually negatively affect the rankings. Now, this isn't to say that excellent reviews will help give an enormous boost, but they won't hurt.

Google also knows that reviews can be faked. So, it's surely got some algorithms in place that look at the trust of the reviewers themselves and various other factors. The whole point? Don't try to fake your reviews. Rather, try to garner honest reviews from your customers by asking them for it. You can also place links to your business listings in your email signature. For example, if you're on Yelp, Google, and Facebook, place links there.

This is a great passive way of asking for reviews without having to be direct and in a customer's face about it. If they see you're on the various Internet outlets, and they're the type of person that likes to leave online reviews, you can be sure that they'll take advantage of that. If not, then it's always in your email signature. And, not only will it keep you honest, but it will also send a clear message to the customers that you're committed to their complete satisfaction.

Other ways of soliciting online reviews include placing

a badge from different service providers onto your site. For example, sites like TripAdvisor and Yelp allow you to place badges on your site. Other services such as the Chamber of Commerce and Better Business Bureaus located in certain regions also provide a similar service. Having badges, which are displayed on your site, shows that you're committed to customer service and that you're looking to garner more online reviews. It helps to build that bridge of trust, which only can help you in the long run.

Do your best to locate the best trust-resources to solicit online reviews for your business. Whether it's TripAdvisor, Yelp, Freelancer, Home Advisor, Angie's List, or any other site, pick two or three that you can focus your efforts on. Send those two or three links to your customers or clients in a bid to solicit as many honest online reviews as you possibly can. And, it goes without saying that you should do your best to ensure that every single one of your customers or clients is satisfied at the end of the day.

Now, we've all seen and heard that SEO doesn't happen overnight. Well, nor do online reviews. It takes time to accumulate them. But, when this is taken seriously, it's something that can help boost your overall ranking on Google's algorithm. It might not be an enormous boost, and it might not get you to the first page of Google's SERPs, but it is going to help. Not only will it help with your organic ranking, but it will also help in driving business through these other trusted resources.

4
CONTENT MARKETING

By now, you understand that trust on the Web is derived through three key factors: age, authority, and content. We've covered the basics of this already in past courses. In *SEO Fundamentals*, we looked at what trust through each of these factors meant. Google derives age from the initial indexing date of the domain, authority is derived from link-share quality and frequency on the Web, and content is derived through the building of high-quality content that provides value.

In the second course, SEO Strategies, we looked further into the trust through the content medium, and just what content marketing meant. We listed some authority sites that could be used to deliver that content, and just what link-bait means, but we didn't focus in on specific tactics for building content that will help boost your visibility on search engines like Google. However, this authority content is going to be your primary source of traffic in the beginning, so focusing on content marketing is going to be key.

Since driving traffic to your personal business site is going to be difficult, authority content has to be the primary focus, especially when you're starting out. This is going to be a huge source of initial visibility. Your goal is going to be to build content on authority sites and promote that content ferociously using the techniques that you've learned in the second course, *SEO Strategies & Tactics*. Now, keep in mind that the content on authority sites is much more immune to backlash from Google. So, by heavily optimizing and promoting content on those pages, you run a much lower risk of being demoted on Google's SERPs.

So, how does this work?

Well, there are a few steps involved here. I'm going to outline the steps first and explain how and why they work. You understand the inner-workings of all of this already from past courses, but let's look at just how we're going to build that content and market it to obtain the best exposure.

1. **Research Long-Tail Keywords** – You're already familiar with this step. We've already gone over the Google Keyword Planner in previous courses. But, in this step, we'll look at how to pick the right keywords that provide the biggest boost in the short and long-term.

2. **Create a Content-Marketing Strategy** – In this step, we'll see just how to come up with a game-plan for building content that will achieve the best results. This will include selecting the right sites to

build your content on, and some key points to consider when coming up with your content.

3. **How to Build Excellent Content to Market** – Our focus here is on Business SEO, so we want to build content that will educate prospective leads and customers on your industry, business, or niche. But, we also want to build content that's going to convert. We'll see what makes excellent content tick, and how to go about building it up from the ground level.

4. **How to Promote your Content to Drive Sales** – The name of the game is profit and sales. We'll see just how to promote that content using some of the strategies and tactics that we picked up from the previous course. This will be an essential part of your success in *SEO for Business*.

STEP 1: RESEARCH LONG-TAIL KEYWORDS

The first step in the process of content marketing is to do the proper research. This involves using a variety of resources such as the Google Keyword Planner and other trend-analysis tools, as discussed in past courses. Trend-analysis will help you in the short term as well as the long term, so it's an important part of the process. Once something is trending, and you're able to successfully promote a popular piece of content leveraging that keyword, you'll garner likes and shares that will help you in the long term, while also providing traffic in the short term.

To get started, you really have to do some brainstorming. If you've put some significant thought into your business already, then this shouldn't be too difficult. Take your business, niche, industry, and target demographic, see just how you can spin it to build content that will be interesting, engaging, and provides value. If you remember some of the key fundamentals from back in the first course, the primary purpose here is to always provide value. Either you're going to entertain or inform; that's where your value is going to come from. If you skimp on the value, then you can forget about reaping the benefits of content marketing.

So, put some thought into this process. Login to the Google Keyword Planner Tool and use some long-tail keywords to help describe what you're targeting. However, you might find it far easier to do this if you engage in a brainstorming activity on paper first. Think about your business. What industry are you in? Who's your target customer? What are they looking for? What questions do they have? If you're in the business of selling home mortgages, what are some of the most common questions that you'll find in that industry? What do your customers usually want to know?

Whether you sell houses, cars, widgets, or information, think about the type and style of questions you would, could, or do usually get from customers. Think about what you find yourself telling them over and over again. Then, set about designing some long-tail keywords to help describe those questions. Maybe you find yourself being asked what the difference is between a fixed-rate mortgage and a variable interest-rate mortgage is. If so, describe that in the form of a long-tail keyword, such as "What's the difference between a fixed-rate and variable interest-rate mortgage?"

Or, maybe you're selling cars and people want to know the real benefits of leasing versus buying. Maybe they want to understand what a lease really is, or the real-money factor involved with leases. Most people don't understand the details in any number of given fields. Your whole goal here is to help provide value by spreading quality information. When you do this on authority sites, you'll find yourself ranking very quickly for these keywords. But you have to think of a good long-tail keyword that will drive traffic to your business by helping to spread that value.

When you do the research for your long-tail keywords, you're looking for the keywords that have the greatest search volume for the lowest competition. Now, I know that Google Keyword Planner Tool is meant more for advertisers and those vying for listings of ads on Google's SERPs. However, it's your best resource for deriving some estimation of the kind of traffic that you could expect. So, find the keywords that work best for you, because only you can determine that. As long as you ensure that you do the proper brainstorming and research first, you won't be wasting your time.

Make sure that you find 5 to 10 excellent ideas for keywords in this step. If you have to, get organized and create a spreadsheet of the keywords, their respective search volumes, competition, and any other metrics you'll want to add on. Later on down the road, you can use Google's Webmaster Tools to see just how you're ranking for the keywords that are giving you visibility. Not only will Google's Webmaster Tools show you the search position for the keywords, but it will also give you the number of impressions and clicks for each of those keywords.

You'll need metrics like Google's Webmaster Tools when you're analyzing your search traffic with all SEO-related activities, so be sure you're already acquainted with it and how it works. You'll also need to submit an XML sitemap and verify that the domain is yours. So, be sure that you do the work early on and be prepared to analyze how well your content marketing goes down the road. Since, without metrics, we're really just crawling around in the dark.

Today, Google Analytics won't provide the full picture anymore due to the "Keyword Not Available," scenario from encrypted and secure searches. So, Google has committed to providing more of the data that's absent in Google Analytics, through its Webmaster Tools. Be sure that you're using both resources for analyzing your incoming traffic to find out how they're arriving at your site, and for finding out what they're doing when they arrive there.

STEP 2: CREATE A CONTENT-MARKETING STRATEGY

Content marketing for business requires a strategy, and it requires being organized in both your work and your time. Why is that? Well, if you recall back from prior courses, you know that Google is very sensitive to the amount and frequency of the links that are created to any site. It knows, especially for brand new sites, if thousands of links are suddenly created, that it's not natural or organic. Now, this isn't to say that something can't go viral and gain traction on Google's SERPs. We discussed a viral-marketing strategy in our last course on *SEO Strategies & Tactics*. What this does say is that you do need a schedule for creating your content.

Why is a schedule important? Well, before we get to the overall content-marketing strategy, let's discuss the scheduling of your content. There are several important factors at play here:

1. Content must be unique
2. Content must provide value
3. Content must not appear spammy
4. Content must be relevant
5. Content must have authority

Now, we've already covered several of these factors in the past. We talked about how content is king, and just how important unique content is that provides value. And, we also discussed the importance of content that's relevant in the sense that it must not go off topic. When you're optimizing for a particular keyword, don't try to vary the subject too much. And, the content must have authority, which comes from either having a high PageRank to begin with, or receiving high PageRank backlinks from authority sites.

So, that leaves us with one last point here: content must not appear spammy. Now, we've covered so much to do with spam content, algorithm adjustments, and Google penalties. But, when it comes to content marketing, the game changes a bit. Why is that? Well, content marketing, when done right, is done on authority sites. Some people mistake that as a carte blanche or free check to do whatever they like. This is not the case. Content marketing through authority sites can still be spammy if the following occurs:

1. **There are too many outbound links** – You

can't crowd content, whether it's on your site or an authority site, with too many outbound links. Outbound links are evidence of spammy content. Focus on one, maybe two total links that are going to relevant content. One of those links, should of course be pointed to your site.

2. **The content isn't well written** – If the content is too short, goes too off topic, has spelling or grammatical errors, or appears to be written by someone who's a non-native speaker, the content will come across as low-quality content. When content is considered low in quality, and only appears to serve an SEO purpose, it might get flagged and removed, by being considered as too spammy.

3. **There is too much similar content being created that's all linking to the same source** – Too many articles are being created that are all similar, which are all linking to the same source. This can raise red flags with Google.

So, when you're creating a content-marketing strategy, you have to be hypersensitive to spammy content. You don't have a blank check to do what you want just because you're marketing on authority sites. In fact, not only do you have to present excellent content, you have to create a schedule of delivering that content on a periodic basis. Whether it's weekly, bi-weekly, or more often, you need to come up with a schedule and stick to it. The reason being is that you won't see much progress from marketing just one piece of content. You need to keep the authority content coming, repeatedly.

Also, you can't deliver too much content too fast. It's far better to market one good piece of content every week, than one subpar piece of content every single day. Remember, it's quality, consistency, and persistence that are going to count here. It's easy to do too much too fast. We also see this when we were discussing some of Google's algorithm adjustments and just how they went after link farms that were pushing out subpar content that was very heavily linked. So much has changed since the heydays of the Web. You have to keep it all in mind when you're optimizing any piece of content.

So, come up with a strategy that works for you, along with a schedule, and stick to it. Research your keywords, and come up with content ideas that you want to market. Create articles, videos, ebooks, tutorials, and anything else you can think of, and stick to a schedule to market it. This isn't going to be easy, and it will involve a lot of your time. However, if you stick to building this content on authority sites, and stay persistent, it will provide the greatest benefits in the short-term and long-term for your time spent.

STEP 3: HOW TO BUILD EXCELLENT CONTENT TO MARKET

Building excellent content isn't easy. If it were, everyone would do it. But, what makes a good piece of content great? What makes content that everyone likes and wants to share, tick? Well, there are a few key points here that you'll need to address. First, you must think about your industry, niche, business, and target customer enough to ask the right questions. If you've done the keyword research, then you have a good idea of the right questions being asked. But how do you pick the best question to craft your content around?

This isn't easy by anyone's standards. It takes hard work and some intuitive thinking to come up with the right thing to write about. However, before you even do that, you have to consider the type of content marketing you want to do. Here are the choices:

1. **An article** – This is your basic content marketing piece. Writing an article about any topic is easy. But, writing a great article is the hard part. If you're not a writer, then you may need to outsource this to someone who is really good. But, if there's one skill that you should develop when it comes to any industry, it's certainly writing. Or, more importantly, copywriting.

2. **A How-To Guide** – This goes a bit further than an article. In fact, a how-to guide is really an educational resource that just about anyone can reference to help educate them on some topic. Are you a realtor? Maybe you want to create a how-to guide about purchasing your first home or qualifying for your first mortgage. If you're a salesperson, maybe you want to create a how-to guide for the product or service that you sell. This can literally be anything, but it has to have excellent presentation and be well-written.

3. **An Infographic** – These have become extremely popular lately. An infographic helps to visually portray some metric or set of statistics. These can be anything from trends, to market segment statistics, or even related to patterns involving finances, careers, relationships, and so on. But, usually, this is going to require a skilled designer's assistance. To make an infographic visually appealing, it really will need to be presented in the best way possible.

4. **Video Tutorial** – Another form of content marketing is in the area of video tutorials. This works best when the video quality is high, however. So, if you've never made a video before, then you might need to get the help of a professional here. Or, you could simply start learning the basics of video shooting and editing yourself. It's entirely up to you. But, again, here you'll have to choose a topic that you can accurately do a tutorial on. And, it still has to provide value and be unique in some way.

5. **Presentation or Slideshow** – This type of content is catchy and has been revolutionizing the Web. Viral sites like SlideShare.net have been fueling this growth, which allows this type of content to gain tremendous amounts of traffic. These presentations are also relatively simple to setup. Most people are familiar with using software like Microsoft's PowerPoint, which is one of the resources available for setting these up. This is a great way to present visual elements in a presentation format without having to write a lengthy article.

Of course, there are other forms of content marketing. Depending upon how much work you want to do, you could write an ebook or some other manual for doing or achieving something. This type of content marketing can spread virally if done right. But this does take an enormous amount of work to achieve. However, if you're like most everyone else, then you'll most likely tackle one of the four items in this list. So, either you're going to do an article, a how-to guide, an infographic, or a video tutorial. You have to pick the one on the list that you think is best suitable for you. Which one you can successfully tackle is entirely up to you. Just set a goal, and go for it.

Once you've decided on the type of content that you want to market, you have to abide by a few rules for creating that content. Now, we've already discussed what makes a piece of content work. We saw the following:

1. Content must be unique

2. Content must provide value

3. Content must not appear spammy

4. Content must be relevant

5. Content must have authority

We looked in depth of how not to make content appear spammy. Making content unique is pretty straightforward: you don't want to copy anything else that's out there. Being unique might be a straightforward point, but it certainly takes lots of work. But what about the other three? How can we provide value, really be relevant, and build up authority with that content? Not easily, that's how. However, you will find these points somewhat similar to the on-site optimization points discussed earlier in this book, and in previous courses.

When you're developing content to market on authority sites, you're still going to have to abide by a certain set of rules. The only difference is that you'll be able to get away with more on authority sites than you could on your own site. Since authority sites have high PageRanks, you can send more links to those sites without a huge risk of being demoted on Google's SERPs. We saw some of these strategies in the last course on *SEO Strategies & Tactics*. But, overall, here's what's involved with content marketing:

1. **The content must be lengthy** – You can't expect to quickly throw something together here and have it rank well. The content has to be lengthy – at least 1000 words – if you expect to get any traction out of it. Now, creating an article, video tutorial, how-to guide, or anything else is hard, especially when you consider that it has to be at least 1000 words or more. Further, staying on topic is even harder for those 1000 or more words. This can get tricky, but you have to focus here. The better the quality of work this is, the more traction you can expect to gain from it.

2. **The content must be keyword-rich** – The content has to not only stay on topic, but also be rich in keywords. Now, if you've learned anything form the past two courses you've learned that this is not a literal meaning, but can also be a figurative one in the sense that we can use LSI keywords. Remember, too much repetition can be cause for alarm by Google, but you also have to ensure that similar keywords are placed in the content that you intend to market. If you don't know what an LSI keyword is, I suggest you go back to the previous two courses for that information.

3. **The content must have high-quality images** – Google places special weight on the quality of an image. If you don't have high-quality images in your content, you're going to get less traction. However, you also have to ensure that you have the proper rights to use those images. If you're serious about content marketing, then I would suggest signing up at one of the stock photography sites such as ShutterStock.com or iStockPhoto.com, or any of the other hundreds of sites out there that provide quality stock photos.

4. **The content must be properly optimized** – You have to ensure that you've optimized the content that you're intending to market. This isn't just about keyword density, but also about optimization of other content elements. This includes headings, image-alt tags, image names, content title, content sectioning, and so on. Some optimization isn't possible on certain authority sites depending upon the nature of the content and the authority site in question. However, it's your responsibility to optimize the content to the best of your ability, based on what you've learned in past courses. Much of the on-site optimization techniques will apply here for the authority content.

5. **The content must have a link to your site** – This goes with that concept of link juice that I introduced in the last course. The authority content can have many links going to it, and as long as it only has one link going out to your site, you've just built a very powerful link-bridge. Also,

while you can have links to other sites and pages on authority content, placing too many links is going to devalue that content. Think about it like a hallway with many doors in it that are locked. As Google comes down the hallway and finds just one door unlocked, that's where it's going to go: your site. If Google finds many doors unlocked, it will realize that the importance of that page isn't just your site, but others as well. This will decrease the value of the link-juice coming from that page.

When you've concocted a plan of what type of content you'll market and how you'll optimize it, then you need to select a resource for posting that content. There are several authority sites, which I discussed in the previous course on *SEO Strategies & Tactics*. Below, I'm listing off the best sites to use depending on the type and style of content that you're marketing. Now, there are other authority sites that can be used as well, but these are some of the most popular ones for their respective content types.

1. **An Article**

    a. Blogger.com

    b. Hubpages.com

    c. LinkedIn.com

    d. Tumblr.com

    e. Wordpress.com

2. **How-To Guide**
    a. Scribd.com
    b. Slideshare.net

3. **Infographic**
    a. Facebook.com
    b. Plus.Google.com
    c. LinkedIn.com
    d. Tumblr.com

4. **Video Tutorial**
    a. Vimeo.com
    b. YouTube.com

5. **Presentation or Slide Show**
    a. Scribd.com
    b. Slideshare.net

BUILDING AUTHORITY IN CONTENT MARKETING

There's no doubt that, by now, you understand just what authority is and how it's built up. You know that building authority for new domains that haven't yet been indexed by Google is difficult. That's because of Google's weariness to trust the newcomers to the Web. If you have a history with the search giant, then this is much simpler to achieve. You'll also recall some of our discussions about aged domains and just why they're so popular. But, authority sites are a completely new level of popularity.

Authority sites are so trusted by Google that, often, you can post content on an authority site that will be ranked within minutes if it's properly optimized. Why? The enormous PageRanks that these sites have instill an inherent trust by Google. Google knows that content coming from these sites can expect to be trusted. Further, if you do just a little bit of link-building to that authority content, tremendous things are bound to happen. In fact, you'll be pleasantly surprised at just how well this method is going to work to help drive traffic, get leads, and eventually, sales for your business.

So, until now, you've most likely researched some keywords, thought about the type of content you wanted to market, selected an authority site, and maybe even begun to craft some content. But, what next? How do we get Google to really recognize that content? Well, considering that the content is coming from an authority site, you're one step ahead of the game. Now all you have to do is build some links to that content. This can be done in a variety of ways, but, primarily, you should follow some of the linking strategies that were presented in the previous course on *SEO Strategies & Tactics*.

So, why do we need to build links to content on authority sites? Isn't it just a given that it will rank high no matter what we do? Well, yes, and no. Content on the authority site will naturally rank higher. For example, if you were to post content on an authority site for a long-tail keyword with little competition you might see it rank immediately on the second or third page of Google. Over time, it might move up to the bottom of the first page. But, you can quicken that process by building some links to the content to help give it a boost.

Your time spent doing this is much more valuable. Why? Well, let's take the discussion back to the previous course again. In the previous course, you saw just how link juice worked and how to create buffers and tiers. Those buffers are the sites that sit between your site and all the incoming links. When those buffers are authority sites, the risk for demotion on Google's SERPs is limited. Since authority sites have a much higher PageRank and are inherently trusted by Google, building dozens or even hundreds of links to them is okay as long as it's done naturally and organically. You simply can't blast a thousand links each day to any site and expect positive results.

So, you need to spend some time building links to that content that you're marketing. And, as long as that content has a single link to your own Website, then all the link juice should transfer over to your site. Take the time to build some quality content with quality links that are diverse. Remember, Google doesn't like to see all the links coming from one place; it likes to see diversification. So, every link shouldn't come from just Facebook, or just Google Plus, and so on. Spread the link love around the Web. That's the best way to get your content to rank better and faster. It's also the best way to drive traffic to your business, get leads, and spur sales early on.

Here are the steps involved with building authority for the content that you intend to market on the Web. This is a one-week plan to build and market content on the Web. If you're confused about any of these steps, please go back to the *SEO Strategies & Tactics* course.

1. **Day 1** – Create your high-quality content with one link to similar content on your own site, or simply to your homepage.

2. **Day 2** – Create 3 to 5 social media links to your content using the leading social media sites. This shouldn't come across spammy. Ensure that whatever you share is adding value, is unique, and is relevant to the people that you're sharing it with.

3. **Day 3** – Purchase 50 to 100 high-quality links from sites like One Hour Back Link or High PR Society and ping those links at a rate of 5 to 10 links per day to Google (see discussions about pinging in past courses).

4. **Day 4** – Create an additional piece of quality content using a secondary source. This one doesn't have to be as high in quality as the original content that you're marketing. This should be done on a site like Wordpress.com, Blogger.com, HubPages.com, or any of the other sites. This shouldn't link directly to your site but directly to the content created on Day 1.

5. **Day 5 to 7** – Use EmpireAvenue or TribePro to incentivize other people to build quality links to your content created on Day 1 and Day 4.

5
BUILDING A SALES FUNNEL

Now that we've touched on some of the fundamental aspects for marketing a business on the Web and driving traffic, let's look at just how to configure a sales funnel. This is going to be the most important part of your business and converting that all-important traffic from prospects, into leads, and into sales. So, how exactly is a sales funnel configured? What does it precisely look like and what are the different components that need to be in place in order to have a proper working funnel?

Well, at the behest, we have the foundation of the site and the business. There has to be value at the core of whatever it is that you're marketing or selling. Whether it's a product, service, or information, the inherent value, not only in what you're pitching has to be there, but also in the information that's being provided for your niche. Once you have the foundational core concepts of value in place, you can move on to building your funnel.

So, let's just look at this scenario: you have a site that's already up and running. You understand what it takes to drive traffic, organically speaking, to that Website based upon what you've learned here in the SEO University and elsewhere. What's it going to take to capitalize on that traffic? Well, for that traffic to be effective, it needs to filter into your sales funnel. And the most important part of a sales funnel is in its ability to convert that traffic into leads and customers. So, what do you have to put into place exactly?

The first and most important thing that you're going to need is a system that you can use to collect email addresses and build your list. Built a list? Wait a moment. I know what you're thinking. "I don't want to spend the time building a spammy email list." But, did you know that, according to ConvinceAndConvert.com, 44% of email recipients made at least one purchase in 2012 based on a promotional email? And, 33% of email recipients open email based on subject line alone?

Yes, the most valuable asset that you're going to have in business is your list. You've most likely heard this before. Your list of email addresses should be treated with the utmost care and respect, and it should never be abused. However, building that list isn't going to be easy. In the beginning, it will be frustrating. But, over time, you'll see your list grow, and you'll have a chance to market to a large and captivated crowd who will have your attention. As long as you don't miscommunicate with them, and you always provide value, you'll see that list responding well.

But, first, you have to collect those email addresses and learn the basics of just what it takes to setup your system. Please note, that you'll have a slight learning curve here. And, this course isn't intended to be an email marketing course, but I will cover the basics. The whole point of this course is to understand just how to drive traffic, but also what to do with the traffic when it arrives. You simply can't just allow the traffic to languish on your site; you need a method for converting prospects to leads, and leads to sales. This will be your sales cycle, and you'll be able to determine some conversion statistics based upon the number of prospects you're able to convert into leads. And later, just how many leads are converted into sales.

So, to get started, let's first look at what system we should use to collect email addresses. Presently, there are three *major* systems available on the market today for email marketing. These three systems will not only allow you to collect those email addresses, but also to conduct email campaigns. All of these systems will help you to comply with federal laws when it comes to SPAM. But, you must also be proactive and ensure that you comply with regulations such as the CAN-SPAM Act. The three major systems are as follows:

1. GetResponse.com – Quite possibly one of the best systems as far as tailoring emails that are time-based, goal-oriented, or simply auto-responding. This company has been around since 1998 and it has a very sophisticated system for building out your contact list, customizing the look-and-feel of email templates, and communicating with your subscriber base. Furthermore, the company offers a 30-day free trial period; afterwards, they offer varying subscription rates based on the number of contacts in your subscriber list. As your subscriber lists grows, you can expect to pay more. However, until you reach 1,000 subscribers on most platforms, you won't have to worry so much about this. For example, currently, GetResponse.com charges $15 US per month for

up to 1,000 subscribers, then $25 per month for up to 2,500 subscribers.

2. AWeber.com – This email marketing company has been around for over 15 years and they are by far a leader in the industry. They provide some of the most cutting-edge tools and are trusted by a wide array of very well known Websites to handle their email marketing campaigns. The system is simple and easy to use. Once you have this system configured optimally, you can confidently expand out your subscriber base by calculating your lead conversion rates. Meaning, for every 100 leads, if 2 people buy something from you, then you can calculate your profitability. If you know your profitability, then you can carefully estimate how much it would cost you to expand out your efforts. For example, this is extremely helpful when using paid marketing to gain more leads. When you know just how much money a lead costs, and that every 100 leads brings in 2 sales, then if you calculate how much money you make from each sale on average, you can effectively calculate your profitability by scaling your marketing.

3. ConstantContact.com – This Company has probably been around the longest of the group. Since 1996, from the dawn of the Web, ConstantConact.com has provided an avenue for mass-email distribution. They have a sophisticated system for communicating with leads and offer some great template options. Feel free to setup an account at all three and take their free trials for a

spin. You might like one more than the other. Everyone has a preference, but all three are terrific providers. However, once you do decide to get started, it's important to stick with one system. You'll want to build out your contact list and familiarize yourself with one of these over the other two.

STEP #1 – SETUP EMAIL SYSTEM

So, the first step in setting up your sales funnel to capture the email addresses of prospects that arrive on your Website is to setup an email system. You'll have to select one of the three systems discussed, and setup an account with them. Of course, the system that you go with is entirely up to you. You can take all three of them for a test-drive, but it's important that you stick with only one to use moving forward. You might select the email system based on the most features or the lowest price, but that decision is entirely up to you. Be sure to give them a thorough test and try out the different features offered. Of course, you might not be able to have a full understanding of what each system is capable of until you begin dropping leads in and sending out emails. So, you can run some tests with your own email address.

At first, this is going to seem foreign to you. Many people like to run businesses and setup shop, but they don't know the first thing about marketing. When you first dip your foot into the pool, it can seem like you're in turbulent waters. You might feel like you're a sinking ship at times, but that's okay. Over time, you'll get the hang of it. Over time, you'll come to understand the importance of email marketing and building a platform of leads and customers for your business. Your list is going to be incredibly valuable to your business so don't abuse it. You'll come to find out more about this later, but for now, keep that golden rule in mind. And, by abusing it, I mean to not sell off your list or over-contact and spam them. These are huge industry noes.

STEP #2 – BUILD YOUR FREE OFFER

Okay, this is the hard part. This is where you get to build out your free offer. What do you want to give away to people? What style of information do you present? Do you give them a free ebook? Maybe it's a free video tutorial? Maybe it's trial access to some system? Well, what you give them is entirely up to you, but it has to be enticing. People aren't going to simply give away their email address for no reason. As you saw me allude to earlier in this course, if people don't perceive value from you, then they won't be willing to share their contact details. And, even if people do perceive value from you, most of them are still unwilling to give out their personal information. So, you have to provide high-quality information. Whatever you do offer as your free offer, it can't be skimpy. Think about over-delivering here rather than under-delivering because this is going to be the first sign to people of just how much value you can offer them.

So, depending on what industry you're in, you should

create some downloadable information that pertains to that industry. This can be anything from a how-to guide, to an industry checklist, or a complete tutorial. Now, keep in mind that you're going to need to write this piece of information. If you're not good at writing, you could potentially outsource this, but it's going to cost you. If you've never done outsourcing before, you should know that there's a cost versus quality scale. The more you pay, the higher the quality you can expect to receive. However, if you're not good at writing, then developing this skill should be at the forefront of your mind. Whether you're writing static content for your site, blogging, or writing copy that helps to sell whatever it is you're peddling, writing is a skill you need to have.

There are hundreds of resources on the Web for improving your writing skills, but the best way to do so, as the Nike slogan goes, is to just do it. By writing daily and blogging, you can help to develop this skill further. As time goes on, your mind will morph and adapt to writing, and your words will get sharper. You'll be able to convey your thoughts much clearer over time. But in the beginning, you might find it hard. However, anything you do for the first time is going to be hard. But, how much do you want to succeed? If you're really committed, then develop writing as a skill, and build out an incredible free offer ebook that will help people solve some need or fill some void in your industry. Teach them something that they don't already know how to do, and do it in detail. And, don't skimp out on them. Deliver huge content that's in an extended format. Shoot for 10,000 words or higher! Yes, it's a lot of content to deliver, but you only have to write it once. If you do it the right way, then this is going to be one of the best weapons in your arsenal for converting prospects into leads.

STEP #3 – BUILDING CONTENT

The third step to your sales funnel, after you have your email system and offer in place, is to build content. Content on the Web is king; you already know that. And, people want to devour really good content, so give that to them. Spend time obsessing over the content that you post on your site and market on content marketing sites. Do the research and write well-written articles that provide value to peoples' lives. Ensure that you spend the time with this and that it sounds good because no one will trust a site that has subpar content.

Oftentimes, it's difficult for us to invest our time in something we don't see immediate returns from. But, as you build the content and articles on your site, trust from the Web community will build. So, no matter what industry you're in, take the time to find out what people are searching for and write about it. This is going to be the biggest consumption of your time.

The content that you put on your site should be interesting, engaging, informative, and provide value. There's that word again: value. You have to provide value at every step along the way. If you try to skimp on the value, people will notice. For example, if you write a good article but it's littered with spelling and grammatical errors, why would anyone want to read more of what you have to offer?

Why would anyone be interested in your free offer and provide you with their email address when you don't even take the time to check your content for errors? They won't. You have to pay attention to the details every step of the way. You have to ensure that you take all the time that's necessary in order to do things the right way; otherwise, you're wasting your time for nothing. People won't care about what you have to say if you don't care about the things you say and how they're said.

STEP #4 – BUILDING YOUR AUTORESPONDERS

Once you have your email system, your offer, and your content in place, the time comes to build your autoresponders. The autoresponders are emails located within your email system that will automatically communicate with your leads once they're in the system. You can indicate when each email goes out and what it says. This will give you a hands-free approach to building your business and putting it on autopilot. You can eventually concentrate on pushing out better and better content over time while your list grows. But, in the beginning, this is going to take some legwork so don't get frustrated.

One of the most important autoresponders is going to be the first email that goes out to people when they subscribe to your list. That email is going to have a link to your free offer or have that free offer attached. This is something you can configure through the email system that you choose to build your list with. You'll have to upload your free offer to some place on your website or domain, which will be accessible through a link in that first email. Remember, you're enticing people to give you their email address in order to get that initial freebie. Once they have it, you'll need to begin communicating with them through the automated system.

The thing that you'll have to come up with is a schedule for communicating with your leads on a periodic basis. For example, each of the three major email systems allow you to setup these autoresponders to go out a certain number of days after the sign-up. The beginning is the most important time for communicating with your leads. Right after they sign up and they receive your free offer, you're still fresh in their minds. As time goes on, other things in their lives pop-up, and you fade into the background. But, you can't overdo it, even in the beginning.

For example, you might want to send out an autoresponder email when they signup, then two days after they sign up, then three days after that, then four days after that, and so on, until you hit about one week. Then, you should only communicate with them when there's something important going on. But, the initial emails should allow you to communicate some value to your email list subscribers, and subsequently, down the road, convert them to sales. However, you shouldn't make the mistake of abusing these email subscribers. It's easy to go overboard, trying to cheerlead whatever you're selling to your newfound subscribership. But stay away from doing that.

People despise this type of email marketing: the kind that repeatedly tries to sell them something without providing value. That's why your free offer in the beginning is so important. Then, you have to follow up that free offer with more value. Don't try to sell in every email, regardless of whatever else you read on the topic of email marketing on the Web. Focus on value, and make selling secondary. For example, if you sell homes or condominiums, send out emails regarding some valuable information in your industry. Maybe you want to discuss the recent increase in home prices in your area, or the decrease in mortgage rates; or, how to best prepare your home for sale, and so on. Make sure you add value all the time, and selling will simply come effortlessly after that.

6
SEO FOR BUSINESS

At the end of the day, everything really boils down to your ability to convert. Driving traffic is one thing – there are several excellent methods for actually getting people to your site. In fact, we've covered so much of that in past courses already. But, the real goal here, when conducting SEO for business, isn't just in getting that traffic to the site; it's also about what happens to that traffic when it actually arrives.

So, first, you need a system for analyzing your traffic. You need to find out who's coming to your site and how they're getting there, how much time they're spending there, what pages they're looking at, and which pages they left the site from. All of this data is available through the sources that we've already discussed in past courses. Systems like Google Analytics, Google's Webmaster Tools, and even Piwik, are all great ways for analyzing your traffic.

However, you also need to be able to convert your traffic in order to generate sales. It doesn't end with just getting the traffic there. Your offer has to be good to get those email addresses, and you have to ensure that you continually provide value in the emails that go out to your subscribers. If you're not focusing on all of those things, then you'll see yourself frustrated in trying to market your business. There are so many different facets involved, that often it can seem rather overwhelming.

So, what are some of the best ways in getting your leads to convert to sales? Let's assume for a moment that you've done everything else here: you've setup your site and optimized it, you've done off-page optimization along with that, and you've begun marketing content and driving traffic, and even setup a free email offer with autoresponders. So, what's next? How do we actually get those leads to convert into sales? What are some of the principles behind marketing for business?

Well, I know that you're here for this specific purpose. Anyone who's in business knows that although you can have a stellar product or service, if no one knows about it, then you're left kicking up dust. But, we also know that marketing is hard. It either takes lots of money or lots of time. And most people only have one or the other. Well-established businesses with large marketing budgets can afford to try many paid avenues out to see what works best. But that's not the case for newcomers. Anytime we launch a business, we're mostly left struggling as we try to get the word out.

That's why understanding the fundamental principles behind marketing on the Web is important. You have to know just how to drive traffic to your site, but then, you also have to skillfully help funnel them to the right place. You want prospects to turn into leads, and eventually into customers. So, if you've followed along up until this point, then you've made some progress. Take any one of the skills required in this industry, on their own, and it's clear to see that it's difficult. Combine them all together, and the feat might seem nearly impossible. But, with a little bit of work every single day, you can progress, slowly but surely.

5 PRINCIPLES TO SELLING ANYTHING

Throughout my books, you'll see me speaking about certain principles when it comes to sales. One of the most interesting parallels that you can draw these days is just how inline these principles have become with Google's view on what makes good content tick. In essence, Google has been moving the Web towards these principles for some time now, but only recently has it accelerated. In the past courses, you saw me speak about the algorithm changes that Google has gone through. Those changes have been the driving force of these principles.

So, why is all of this important? This is a book about SEO for Business after all, but why do we care so much about the principles involved with selling on the Web? Don't we just care about getting the people the site and figuring the rest out afterwards? Well, no, that certainly isn't the only case. In fact, these same principles are the same foundational principles that make excellent content rank so high on the Web today. So, let's take a brief look at what these principles are and how we can implement them in our marketing strategies:

1. **Always add value** – You'll notice the parallels here to the world of SEO, since adding value is so important on the Web. But, it's also important in real life. If you have a product, service, or some information that you're selling, you must be adding value in some way or another. And, it must be an exceedingly high amount of value. If the value proposition isn't there, no one is going to listen to you. So, don't expect to do the least amount of work and get the most amount of gain from it. If you don't add lots of value, people will simply brush you aside. There's simply too much competition in business and on the Web for you not to abide by this principle.

2. **Always be unique** – Just like the copycats on the Web, you don't want to appear like you're ripping something off. Whether that's content, a product, a service, or information, you absolutely must be unique. The more unique you are, the better. Think about companies that have unique offerings, which allowed them to get ahead. When PayPal was first introduced, the service was unique. So was Hotmail, another unique service at the time. In New York, there's a donut shop selling "cronuts," which are a cross between a croissant and a doughnut that became wildly successful. Whatever you're selling, try to find a way that you can make your offering unique. If you can't be absolutely unique, you must excel in other areas, but you absolutely should make sure

that you're not exactly duplicating someone else out there. Whatever you do, give it your own unique spin. In the Google World, we know that uniqueness also applies to content. Never copy content, and always come up with something unique that also adds value.

3. **Always be relevant** – It's easy to become irrelevant, or even obsolete. This has happened since the dawn of time. From the industrial revolution to the digital revolution, businesses have fallen irrelevant over time. You must be nimble enough to reinvent yourself or your offerings if you find that you're becoming irrelevant. And, in order to stay relevant, you have to ensure that you're visible. So, you have to find the medium that works for you, in order to make it work. If we're talking brick-and-mortar, things like shop signage, awnings, billboards, and so on determine your visibility. However, in the digital age, we're talking about visibility on the Web through mediums like social medium, blogs, forums, and so on. You have to be relevant by first being visible, then by presenting relevant information to your crowd. For example, you can't talk about a bike repair shop in an aviation enthusiasts' forum. You have to be relevant, always.

4. **Always be consistent** – Whatever you're offering – product, service, or information – you have to be consistent. People like consistency in their lives. If you promise to deliver something, make sure that you deliver it on time, always. You can

quickly lose peoples' trust by being inconsistent. You can't expect the good word to spread about whatever you're selling if you can't remain consistent. So, if you're blogging, stick to a consistent schedule. If you're selling widgets, make sure that you deliver as promised always, on time and on budget. Same thing goes for service offerings. Always provide a high amount of value consistently, and do it repeatedly.

5. **Always build trust** – We've seen how important it is to build trust with Google. Trust is at the heart of SEO, but it's also at the heart of business as well. Over time, you must build trust, not work on ruining it. We've seen how trust can be ruined in the SEO world, but it can easily happen in the real-world as well. In fact, both worlds can spill into one another. Today, with social media, online reviews, forums, and blog commenting, word spreads almost instantaneously. If you want to succeed in business, you simply can't violate your customers' trust and expect to flourish in whatever it is that you're doing.

Understanding these principles in the business world isn't difficult. In fact, if you've learned anything from SEO, then you'll know that these are some of the core principles that you need to abide by. But, understanding these principles, and actually putting them into place are two different things. For example, it's easy to talk about adding value, but when it comes down to it, it can be incredibly hard. It takes a tremendous amount of work to add value, be unique, and be relevant, on a consistent basis, while also building trust.

But, that's just what it takes if you want to convert. You have to abide by these principles, and do it consistently over time, building trust as you go. The more trust you build, the more likely you are to convert your prospects into leads, and your leads into customers. It's relatively straightforward. However, where most people get sidetracked is in the amount of time it takes for some of these efforts to pay off. That's where content marketing comes into play. If you're simply trying to optimize your site, unless you have years of previous indexing by Google under your belt, it will take an excruciating amount of time and work.

The goal here is to drive traffic to your content, which will then help to filter to your site. Even if the traffic doesn't filter to your site, the fact that you'll have a single, solitary link back to your site from that content will help you immensely. So, don't forget about that all-important backlink. It's going to be important in order to drive the traffic. But it's also important to come up with a good strategy for email marketing. This is going to be your ticket to long-term success as long as you don't abuse your list. If you start to abuse your list, then you'll see them begin to unsubscribe. You absolutely don't want that to happen.

7
SOCIAL MEDIA MARKETING

Social media marketing adds another layer of complexity to an already complex recipe to success in the online business world. Not only must you be able to organically optimize your site, engage in content marketing, build trust through online reviews, conduct email-marketing campaigns, and analyze your traffic and statistics, but you must also learn and master the art of social media marketing. Now, if you're not a social person, this might seem like a daunting task. But, there's no way around it. Social media is here to stay, and the high PageRanks of social media sites demand our attention.

So, where do we begin? Well, the first and most important thing that you'll need to conceive is a strategy for moving forward. You have to think about the major social media sites, and just how you want to leverage them. Now, if you've gone through the first two courses, then you've most likely already engaged in some social media marketing. It's a natural occurrence when you're doing

SEO, since using sites like Facebook, Google Plus, and LinkedIn, offer those high PageRank backlinks we're all going after. But, that doesn't give you a full-blown strategy.

When it comes to SEO for business, we not only need a long-term strategy that comes along with any optimization efforts, but a short-term strategy as well. You have to deliver value to your friends, followers, and fans, and do it consistently, without overselling yourself. You have to walk that fine-line between providing that value, and not overdoing. We've all seen those people out there cheerleading whatever it is that they're selling, and do so repeatedly. It can get frustrating to watch this unfold, right?

So, in order to be successful in business, your social media marketing can't come across forced. You can't shove a spoon down peoples' throats with links to your offers multiple times each day. You have to provide value, and make selling secondary. I know, it sounds a little bit counter-productive, doesn't it? But, think about it yourself for a moment. I know that you've seen certain people, businesses, or pages on social media that seem to add a tremendous amount of value to our lives. They post interesting and informative information that's inherently steeped in value. This makes it impossible for people not to like and share that information.

You have to follow along with this value-added approach yourself. This is why you need a strategy at the outset. Sure, links to your pages and posts will help you with SEO, but how about posting valuable information directly on social media? This must be part of the overall plan, because without this, it becomes much harder to build traction early on. And, having a further social media strategy is important as well. For example, several sites are dedicated to online marketers who're looking to help each other spread links in the social media world.

BUILDING A SOCIAL MEDIA STRATEGY

In the last course, SEO Strategies & Tactics, we took a brief look at social signals. We discussed some tools and online resources that can be used in conjunction with an overall SEO strategy. We talked about sites like EmpireAvenue, TribePro, and Fiverr, and how to capitalize on the wealth of resources that these sites provide. And we also looked at two of the SEO strategies employing social signals: link pyramids and tiered-linking structures.

However, that chapter was relatively brief, and more geared towards implementing social media signals in an overall SEO strategy, and not towards how to govern yourself through social media for maximum benefits. When we talk about a social media strategy, we're really talking about spreading value to an active and engaged audience. Unlike blogging for most of the world who don't have thousands of active followers, social media allows you to start a conversation with people. How we govern ourselves in that interaction, has much to do with our potential for success there.

If you're not a social person, don't worry, because you don't have to be. You don't have to invite all of your existing friends on Facebook to join your Facebook Business Page; but it doesn't hurt. What you do have to understand are not only the fundamental principles to interacting on social media, but also the stages of interaction involved. The five principles are an extension of the 5 principles to selling anything on the Web:

1. **Value** – All of your interactions must have some form of value in them – whether informational value or entertainment value – in order to be successful. For example, posts that will help inform, inspire, educate, or entertain people on a certain topic, place, business, niche, event, or idea, should be your primary aim.

2. **Uniqueness** – The majority of your interactions must involve unique content or information. If the content isn't unique to you, you should spread unique information quickly, thus creating authority. Using tools like Google News Alert can help you to achieve this goal.

3. **Relevancy** – Your interactions must be relevant to your fans, followers, or friends. Constantly posting irrelevant posts will result in unhappy people who discontinue following or liking your page. For example, if you're in the business of

selling real estate, ensure that you post about the housing market, mortgage market, and so on, in your area. Don't veer far off-topic.

4. **Consistency** – You have to stay consistent in social media. Don't post once every day for a week then stop for several weeks. Consistency is going to help spur your growth. Further, by being inconsistent, you're sure to lose friends, followers, and fans everywhere on the Web.

5. **Trust** – All of your interactions must be trust-based. Don't try to trick or swindle your friends, followers, or fans. For example, don't try to post articles containing link-bait titles, with the goal of tricking people into clicking on it. Always do things from an honest perspective.

Now that you understand how these principles come into play, you can see how the extension of Google's desires not only stretches into the business world, but also into the social media world as well. That's because these basic principles should be at the foundation of all that you do, not only on the Web, but in the real-world as well. But, beyond these principles, in order to form a proper social media strategy, you have to do the following:

1. **Attract** – This runs parallel to the first principle for selling anything: value. By providing value, you'll attract potential friends, followers, and fans. By not providing value, you're sure to miss out on

many opportunities to make strides in the social media world.

2. **Engage** – When you're interacting on social media, you can't post something and walk away. You have to engage with people. For example, if you were speaking to a group of people, you wouldn't make a statement, and then suddenly leave, would you?

3. **Connect** – It's not always about business. Social media is about connecting. And, any successful social media strategy will involve connecting on a deeper level. Share some intimate detail every once in a while. It will bring the human side of you out.

4. **Convert** – This is where social media fans, friends, and followers are converted into paying customers. This is the ultimate goal, but it shouldn't be the only goal. Social media is a means to an end, but if you focus solely on the bottom dollar, you'll fail.

5. **Retain** – This is inline with consistency and trust in the 5 principles of selling anything. You have to retain your social media friends, fans, and followers by being consistent and not doing things to break their trust. This is an important part of any strategy.

Now, your goal is to come up with a strategy that interlaces the 5 principles of selling anything on the Web, along with the 5 stages of interaction on social media. So, how is this done exactly? Well, first, you have to pick the social media outlets that you want to focus on. There are a tremendous amount of social media sites on the Web, but only a handful that are used by the majority of people out there.

Here are the steps involved with building your own social media strategy. Keep in mind that you have to abide by the 5 selling principles and stages of interaction.

1. **Create a Page** – This involves creating a page for your business. This can be done on Facebook, Twitter, Google Plus, LinkedIn, and just about anywhere else. Remember our discussion about keywords in titles? Well, this will come in very handy when approaching social media. Ensure that you pick a keyword-rich name that will help to increase your overall exposure on the Web.

2. **Promote your Page** – Getting friends, fans, and followers in the beginning is difficult. But you have to start somewhere. Often, the best strategy in the beginning is to do a small promotion of your page to gain friends, fans, or followers. Once you have a small following, you can transition to purely organic marketing. However, this doesn't mean buying fake friends, followers, or fans. You have to use the promotion tools provided by any of these social media sites.

3. **Post Regularly** – Once you have a small following, you have to begin posting regularly. Your posts should be of value, unique, and relevant. Posting regularly helps to breed consistency. And, over time, it helps to develop trust. Remember, all of your posts shouldn't be about sales and promotion. Take the time to help educate and empower your following, and make sales seem secondary. Keep in mind that no one wants to be pitched to on a daily basis.

You have to come up with a schedule for conducting your social media activities that works for you. This doesn't involve wasting time on social media sites, but more so with interacting and connecting with people. Concentrate on spreading value by posting regularly, and ensure that all your posts aren't self-promotion posts. Spread value by posting at least once per day, and stagger your self-promotion posts to every three or four days. This way, you're not overdoing it. Come up with a strategy that works and stick to it. Social media marketing takes time, but it's a very quick resource to help drive prospects to your site, convert them to leads, and eventually, make sales. But it won't happen overnight.

8
VIDEO MARKETING

One of the biggest components to a successful strategy in SEO is video marketing. This is somewhat akin to content marketing, where we briefly discussed video tutorials. But, if you've learned anything about SEO up until this point, then you know just how powerful those short videos on YouTube or Vimeo can be for PageRank and authority. A single link from these online behemoths can give an enormous push to just about any site, no matter how big or small it may be.

However, you have to keep in mind that one video isn't going to cut it. First, that video must be properly optimized. Second, you have to think in larger numbers. For example, if you're selling educational toys, you can't simply write one article, create one video, and expect to be an overnight success. You have to constantly create content that's linked to other great content from authority sites. This is all part of content marketing. But, when the medium is online video, your progress goes into hyperdrive.

So, where do we begin? Well, if you've never conducted any video marketing before, you have some work ahead of you. But, most likely, you've at least dabbled. But, let's first look at why video is so important, then at some strategies for approaching your video marketing exercises. Video, unlike other formats, conveys information using not only visual imagery, but also rich audio as well. The combination of these two help to convey the content more fluidly, along with the expected emotion its intended to carry.

Currently, writing articles or posting pictures on a Website can only get you so far. It doesn't pack the same value-punch that videos do. First, the power of peripheral motion is inherent, since it's part of our anthropological DNA. Videos offer movement, sound, and visual stimulus that's lacking in stale and static content on the Web. It's also been proven that marketing respondents are most likely to react to videos than nearly all other content formats, just behind a learn more or contact us button on a Website. Videos rank higher than white papers, case studies, live-demos with reps, price quotes, webinars, surveys, free trials, and ebooks.

Videos also help to convey emotion unlike any other format that's out there. If you're passionate about something, it comes clearly across in a video presentation. People are much more able to understand you, when they can see you or hear you. Even if you're reluctant to physically appear on the camera, you can use software like Screencast to overlay photos or do some other type of tutorial while you speak. As long as your voice is passionate, you can use the power of video marketing to easily sell whatever it is that you're peddling far easier. It all just boils down to trial and error. You might not get the results you want in the beginning, but you just have to realize it's going to take time.

Video marketing, like SEO, has a learning curve. If you're not up for learning and understanding how to shoot high-quality videos, then you might want to find some help. But, today, just about every laptop or computer has powerful video-editing software. If you're committed to it, you can most certainly find a way to create videos that help to provide value, build you up as an authority, and ultimately, drive prospects into leads, and leads into sales. Plus, it's a great way to help funnel those prospects into your sales funnel.

VIDEO MARKETING STRATEGY

Video marketing requires doing some legwork in the beginning. You can't simply point and shoot. You have to have a plan laid out ahead of time. Now, if you've already been doing some keyword research to help drive that local SEO to your site, then you have some keywords already selected. Creating videos is a powerful way to hit the top of Google's search results, but be sure that your video adds value, and isn't just something that came off as an afterthought.

Here are the five steps to building a video-marketing strategy to help boost your business and drive traffic now rather than having to wait years and years.

1. **Brainstorm an Idea** – Excellent content always ranks highest. Today, even online videos have to feature excellent content. Come up with some

great ideas, or a video series that would be a combination of many ideas, and execute it with precision.

2. **Select a Site** – Choose a site to host your video. You can use some of the usual suspects, but you can also choose social media sites as well. The choice is entirely up to you.

    a. YouTube

    b. Vimeo

    c. Amazon

    d. Tumblr.com

3. **Choose keywords** – The title is one of the most important parts of an online video. Make sure that you choose a keyword-rich title that will help to drive traffic by quickly ranking on Google's SERPs.

4. **Descriptions and link**s – It's important that you place a thorough keyword-rich description in your videos that leads with a link. Links are very important, since links from YouTube and other video sites carry significant weight. You should also consider placing the link or pop-up boxes within the video itself.

5. **Transcripts** – Transcripts are an important part of videos. They help to rank the content within the video quickly. You can build transcripts for online videos in places like YouTube. Make sure that you don't skip out on this very important step.

6. **Link Building** – Once your video is complete, you need to build some links to it. By building authority, you can skyrocket that video to the top of Google's SERPs. Remember, you're already starting out with a high PageRank site. As long as your content is excellent, you can rank that video very quickly with some simple link building. Be sure to reference the *SEO Strategies & Tactics* course for some link-building blueprints.

9
SUCCEEDING WITH SEO

When you're a big company with a sizeable marketing budget, focusing on organic marketing takes a backseat to your paid-advertising endeavors. But, when you're a new business just trying to get the word out, you need every advantage you can get. That's where SEO comes into play. By now, you're familiar with the advantages of sourcing customers through organic-search marketing. People have a tendency to trust the top few listings on Google's SERPs much more than they would say a paid advertisement on the same page.

Still, getting those top placements is hard. As we've seen, it takes the melding of multiple facets in online marketing in order to achieve positive results. But, what's most common is that people give up early on. Most people don't last two or three years of hardcore organic marketing in order to see the fruits of their labors through SEO. In fact, most people give up before their first year is out. However, when you focus on the avenues that drive the most traffic, help to create the most leads, and results in the most overall sales, SEO isn't your only ticket to profitability.

SEO is simply one means to an end. But getting to that end can often feel like such an uphill battle, that most people simply end up giving up the fight. But it's important not to get discouraged. You need to make a plan, get organized, and stay persistent. It's easy to say, but far harder to do. However, you simply have to find a system that works well for you, and don't be afraid to try different approaches. The more you try, the more likely you'll be to succeed, but it's going to take time.

The other very important thing that you have to do is to analyze and track your results meticulously. Make sure that you setup a spreadsheet with your keywords, and track the results over time. Create columns for the number of links you created, when you created them, and what sites you created them on. You have to track with great detail if you want to accurately determine your success. And, ensure that you create a daily to-do list of action items. The more organized you get, the more likely you'll be to follow through. The less organized you are, the less likely you'll be to succeed.

In SEO, often, people want others to do the work. That's because it's incredibly hard. But, if you followed along with this course, then you have a plan of attack for getting your business up and running. Don't be afraid to try things and fail, because it's all part of eventual success. You're going to run into a few brick walls before you can find the path that will lead you to profitability. Before then, don't give up if you hit some stumbling blocks. If you suffer setbacks and you fall down, simply pick yourself back up and try again. It's all part of the learning curve of life.

SEO FOR BUSINESS

The worst thing that you can do is to simply give up because you didn't get the results you wanted overnight. You must realize that SEO for business, for blogging, or for anything else on the Web, is a highly-sought-after skill, and everything you learn now is going to be immensely beneficial to you. So, stick with it and be relentless. Dig your heels in for the long haul and tough it out. You have a long road ahead of you, but there's light at the end of the tunnel. Eventually, day-by-day, you'll make more and more progress. And, as long as you don't throw in that proverbial towel, you will succeed. It just takes time. But,

OTHER COURSES

I hope that you enjoyed reading the material covered in this course. Hopefully, you've come to understand SEO for Business a bit better, and I hope that you've taken away some valuable insight from this course. Keep in mind that your SEO work doesn't end here. Being such a wide, diverse, and evolving field, it's always important that you keep up-to-date with the information being offered. However, this course should have provided you with a general understanding of just how to propel your business forward, turn prospects into leads, and leads into sales.

Be sure to continue your SEO education and look at some of the other courses that are available in this series. From building niche Websites, to content marketing, video marketing, and everything in between, we'll cover some of the advanced strategies for propelling you forward in the SEO world. Remember, there's nothing better than free organic traffic, and there's no other better way to develop that free traffic than truly understanding the world of SEO.

www.ingramcontent.com/pod-product-compliance
Lightning Source LLC
Chambersburg PA
CBHW071800200526
45167CB00017B/552